© Copyright 2021 - All rights reserved.

You may not reproduce, duplicate or send the contents of this book without direct written permission from the author. You cannot hereby despite any circumstance blame the publisher or hold him or her to legal responsibility for any reparation, compensations, or monetary forfeiture owing to the information included herein, either in a direct or an indirect way.

Legal Notice: This book has copyright protection. You can use the book for personal purpose. You should not sell, use, alter, distribute, quote, take excerpts or paraphrase in part or whole the material contained in this book without obtaining the permission of the author first.

Disclaimer Notice: You must take note that the information in this document is for casual reading and entertainment purposes only. We have made every attempt to provide accurate, up to date and reliable information.We do not express or imply guarantees of any kind. The persons who read admit that the writer is not occupied in giving legal, financial, medical or other advice. We put this book content by sourcing various places.

Please consult a licensed professional before you try any techniques shown in this book. By going through this document, the book lover comes to an agreement that under no situation is the author accountable for any forfeiture, direct or indirect, which they may incur because of the use of material contained in this document, including, but not limited to, —errors, omissions, or inaccuracies.

Published by WorldWide Spark Publish

Introduction

Thank you for purchasing this book!

Start your day with a boost of motivation and inspiration, choose to read a daily inspirational quotes that contributes to your well-being.

Your Daily Motivational Quote
Day 1

"How to be happy: decide every morning that you're in a good mood!" -unknown

Your Daily Motivational Quote
Day 2

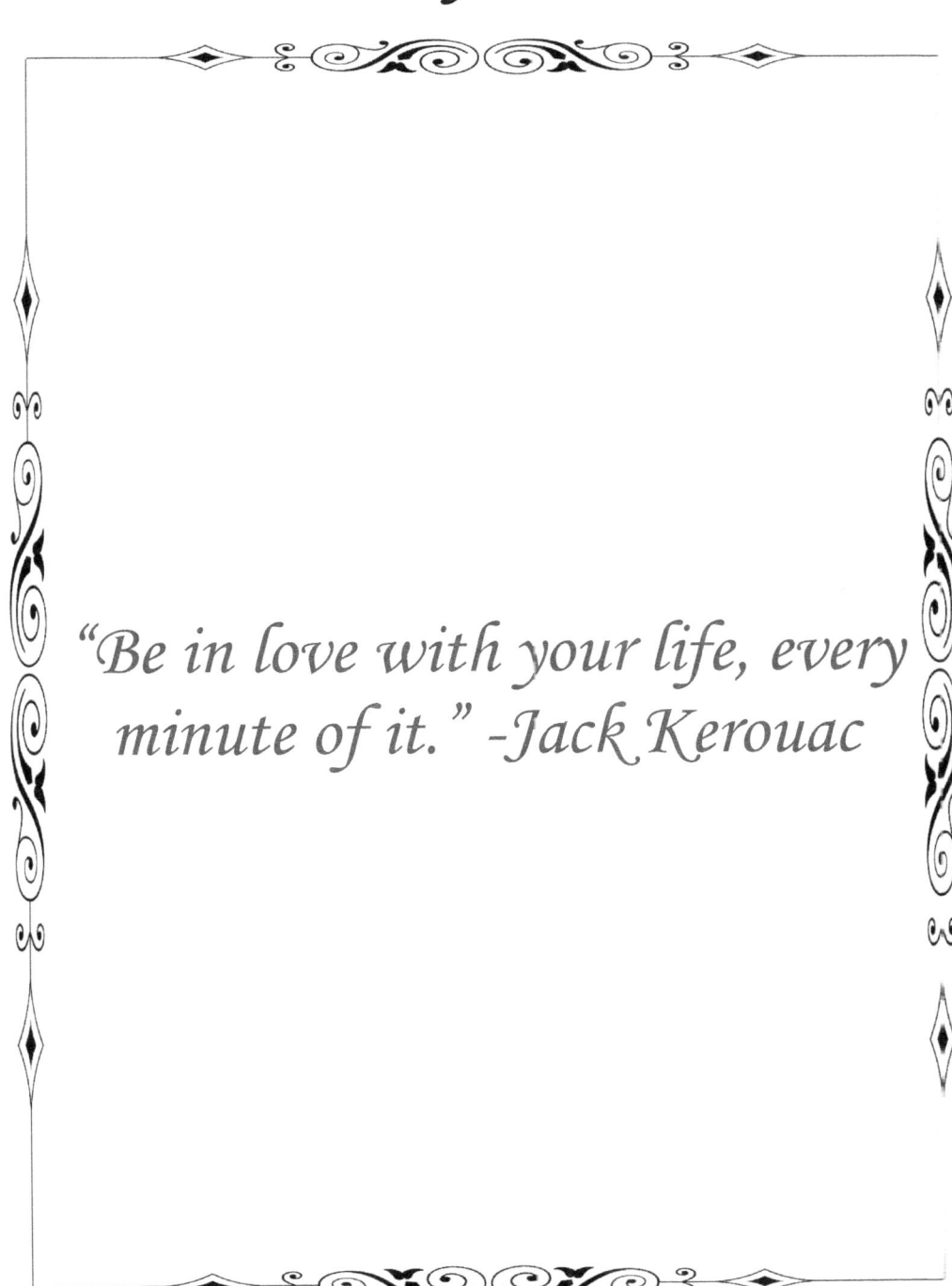

"Be in love with your life, every minute of it." -Jack Kerouac

Your Daily Motivational Quote
Day 3

"A good example is like a bell that calls many to church." - proverb

Your Daily Motivational Quote
Day 4

"The purpose of our lives is to be happy." -Dalai Lama

Your Daily Motivational Quote
Day 5

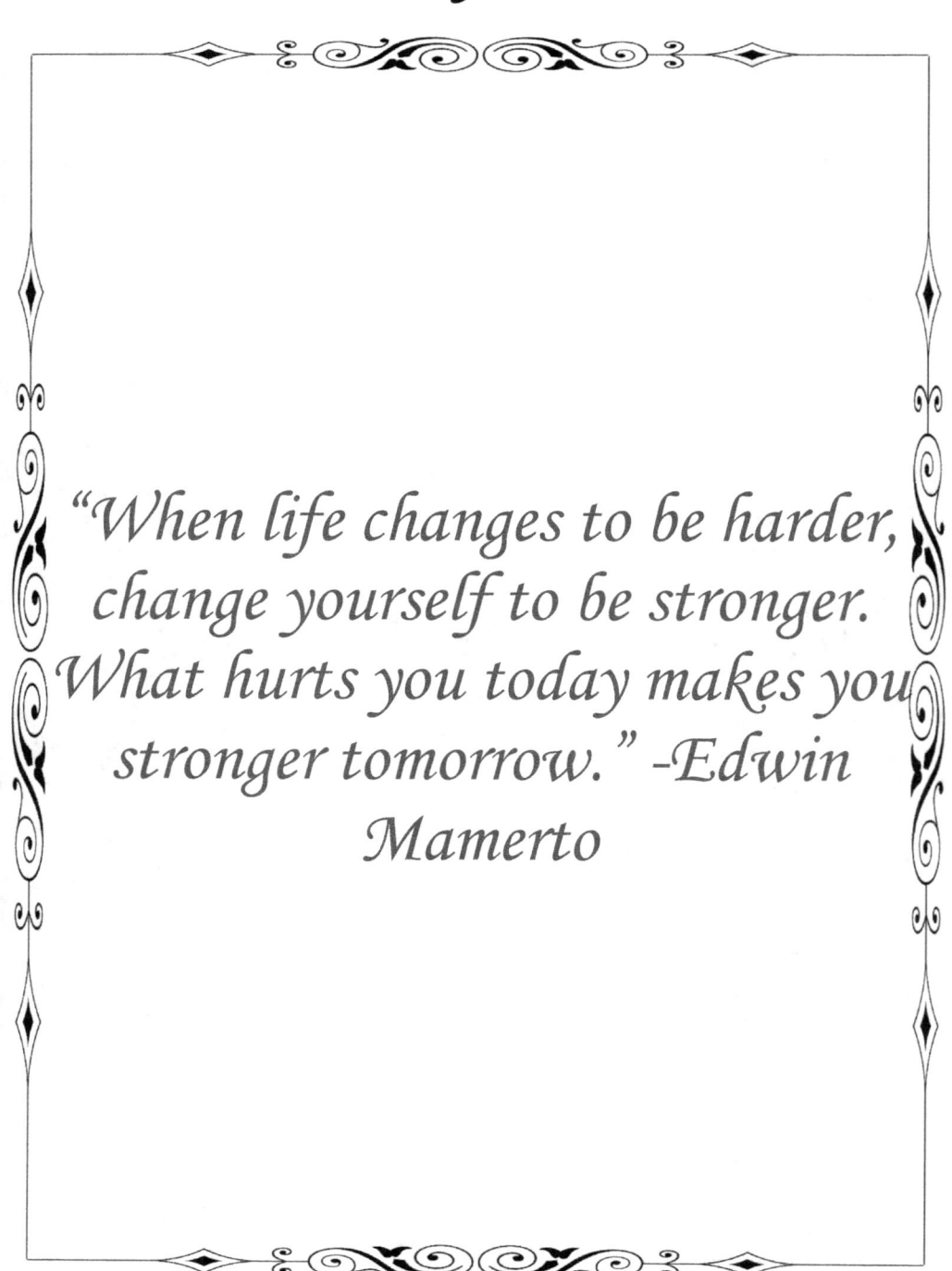

"When life changes to be harder, change yourself to be stronger. What hurts you today makes you stronger tomorrow." -Edwin Mamerto

Your Daily Motivational Quote
Day 6

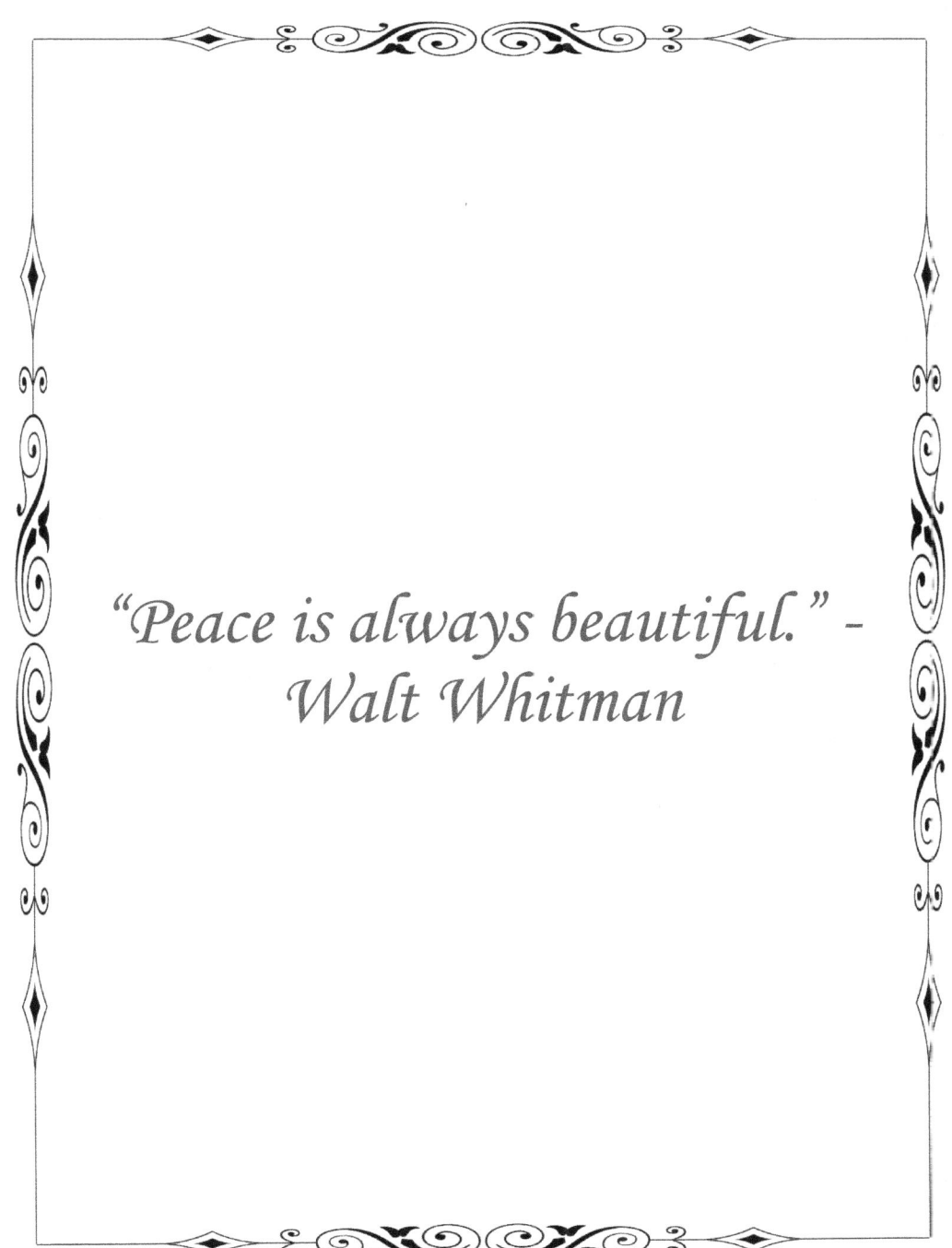

"Peace is always beautiful." - Walt Whitman

Your Daily Motivational Quote
Day 7

"Perspective is the way we see things when we look at them from a certain distance and it allows us to appreciate their true value." -Rafael E. Pino

Your Daily Motivational Quote
Day 8

"I like to be a free spirit. Some don't like that, but that's the way I am." -Princess Diana

Your Daily Motivational Quote
Day 9

"Keep your face always towards the sunshine and the shadows will fall behind you." -Walt Whitman

Your Daily Motivational Quote
Day 10

"If there is magic on this planet, it is contained in water." -Loren Eiseley

Your Daily Motivational Quote
Day 11

"Wake up with a smile and go after life." -Joe Knapp

Your Daily Motivational Quote
Day 12

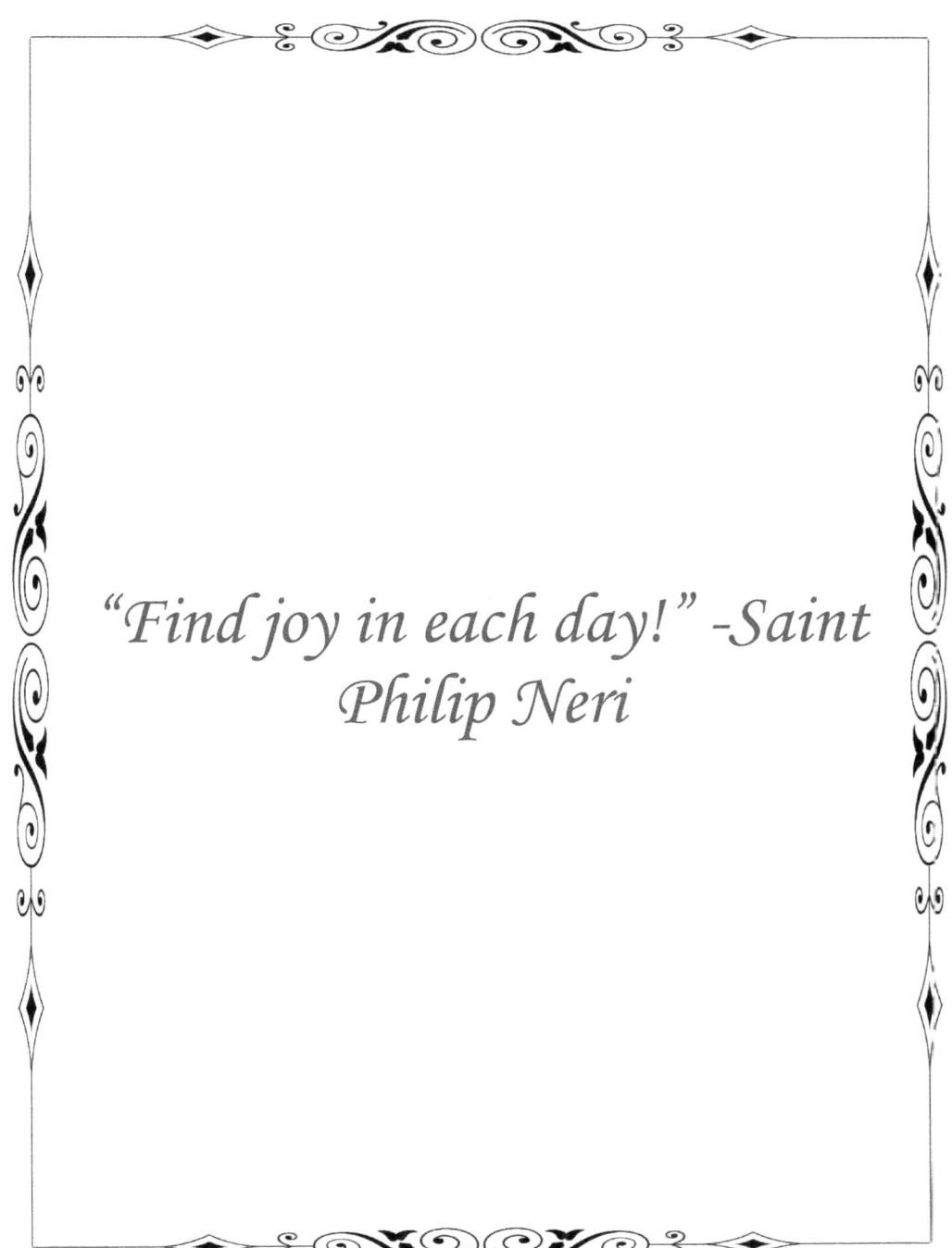

"Find joy in each day!" -Saint Philip Neri

Your Daily Motivational Quote
Day 13

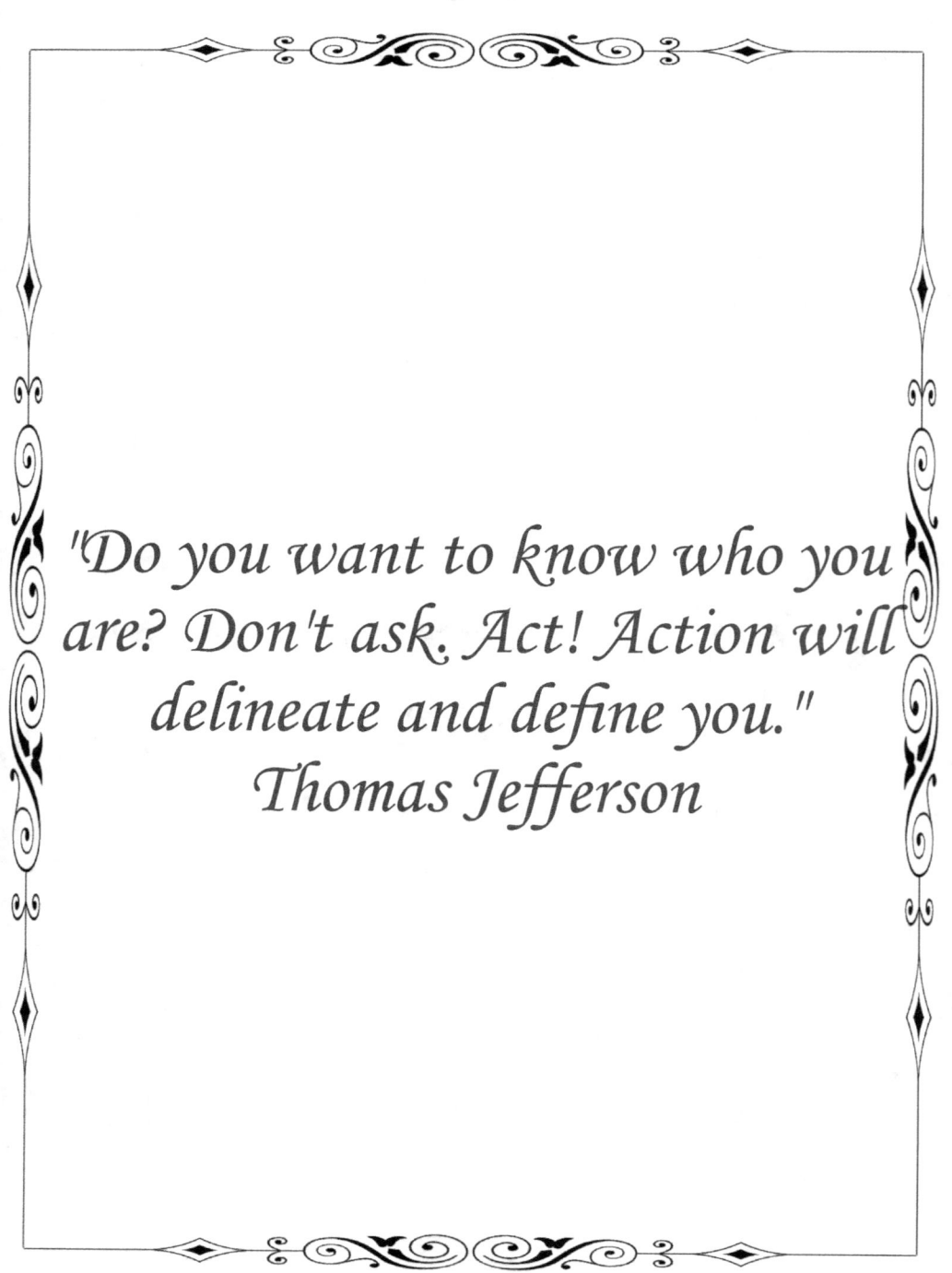

"Do you want to know who you are? Don't ask. Act! Action will delineate and define you."
Thomas Jefferson

Your Daily Motivational Quote
Day 14

"Today is yours to shape. Create a masterpiece." -Steve Maraboli

Your Daily Motivational Quote
Day 15

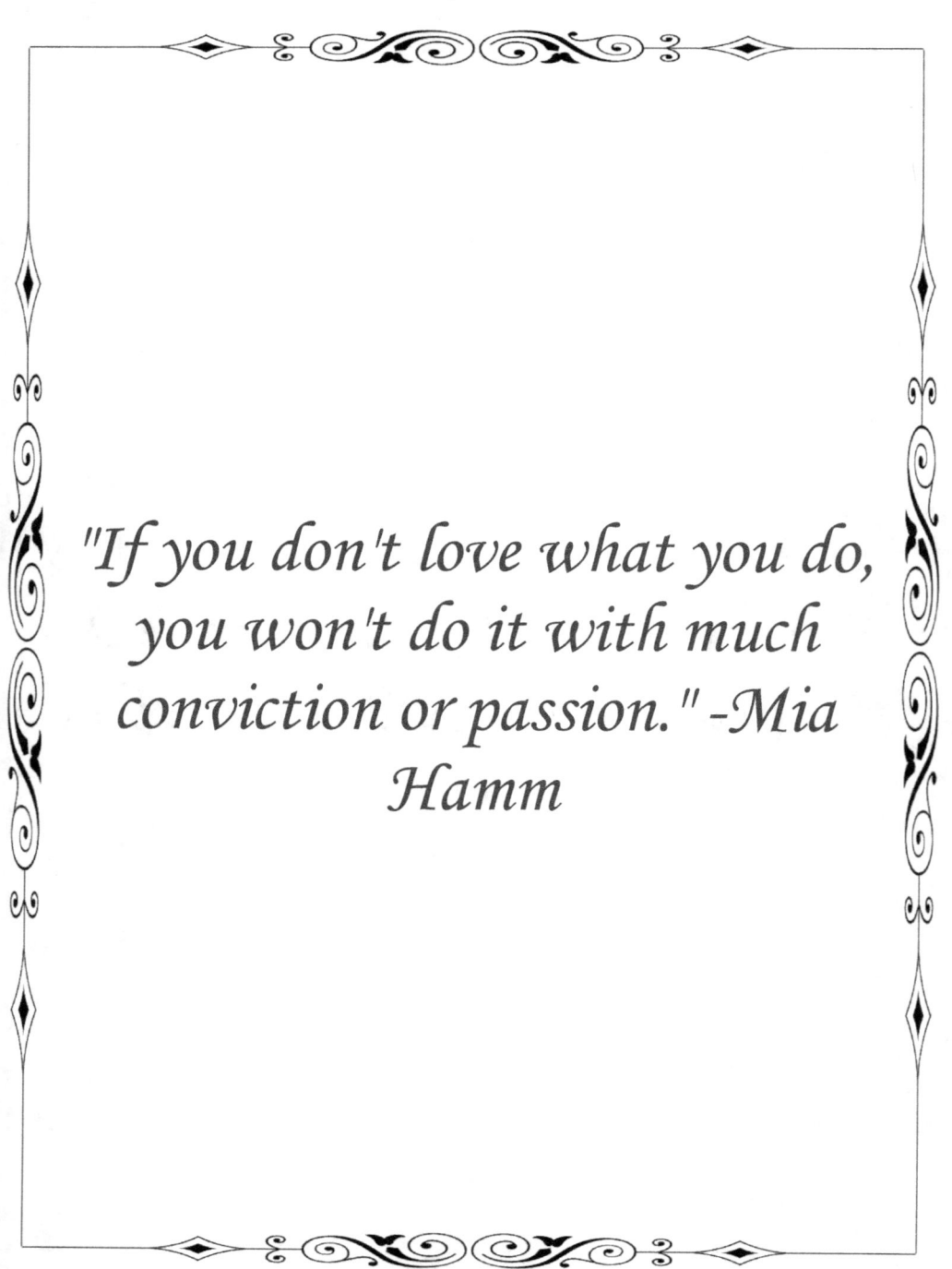

"If you don't love what you do, you won't do it with much conviction or passion." -Mia Hamm

Your Daily Motivational Quote
Day 16

"Cherish your human connections-your relationships with friends and family." - Barbara Bush

Your Daily Motivational Quote
Day 17

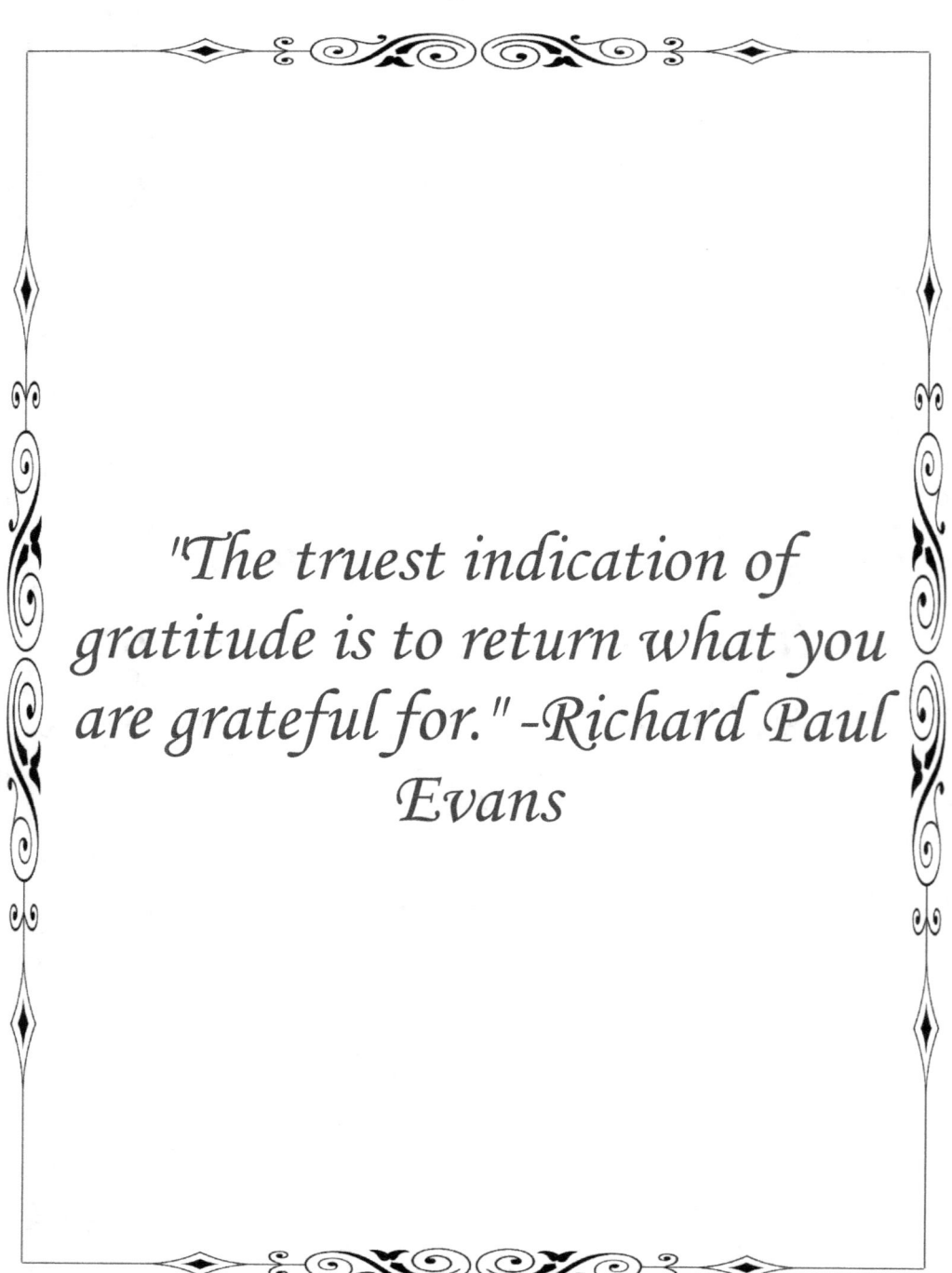

"The truest indication of gratitude is to return what you are grateful for." -Richard Paul Evans

Your Daily Motivational Quote
Day 18

"Humility is really important because it keeps you fresh and new." -Steven Tyler

Your Daily Motivational Quote
Day 19

"We sometimes underestimate the influence of little things." - Charles W. Chesnutt

Your Daily Motivational Quote
Day 20

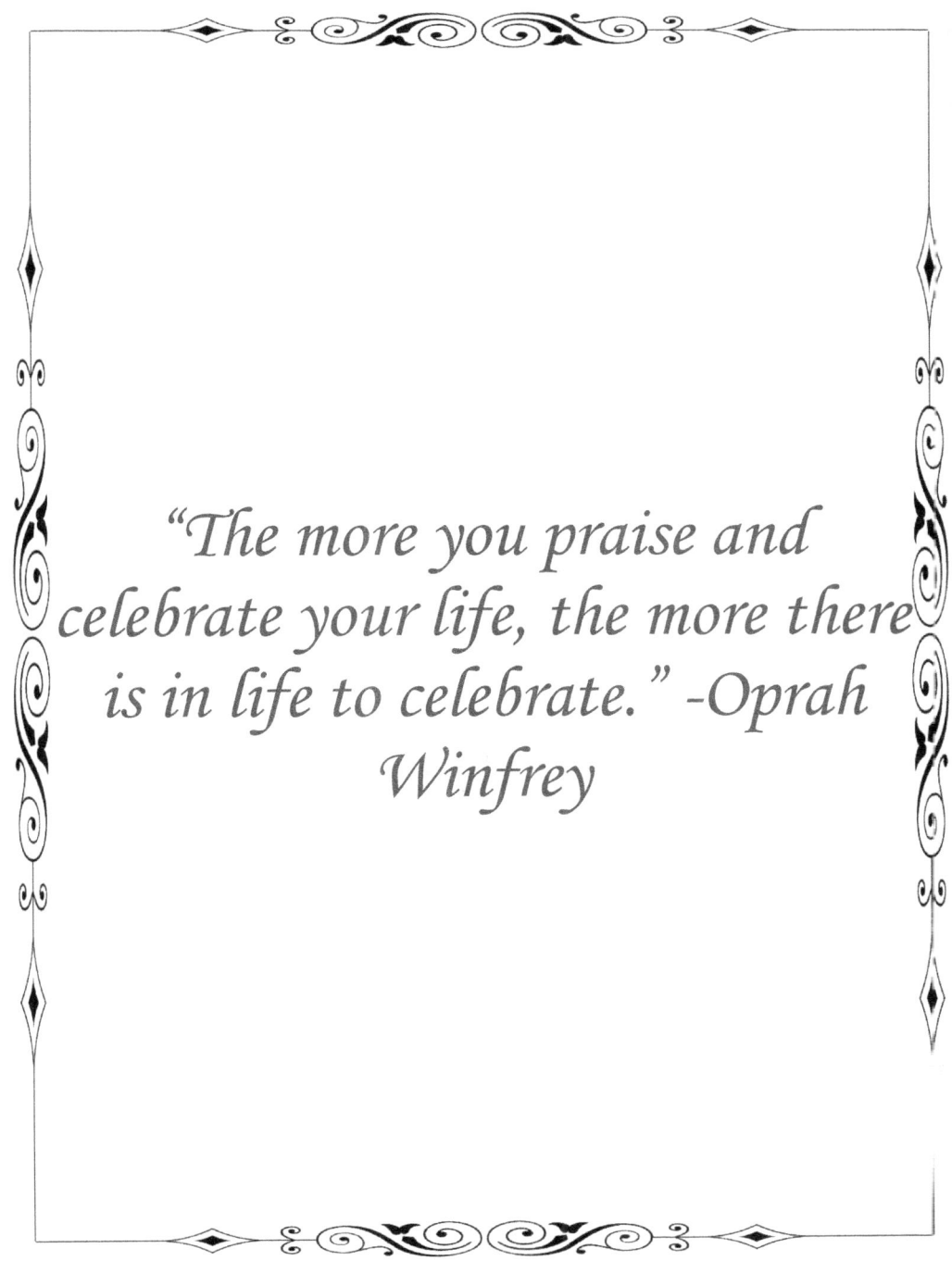

"The more you praise and celebrate your life, the more there is in life to celebrate." -Oprah Winfrey

Your Daily Motivational Quote
Day 21

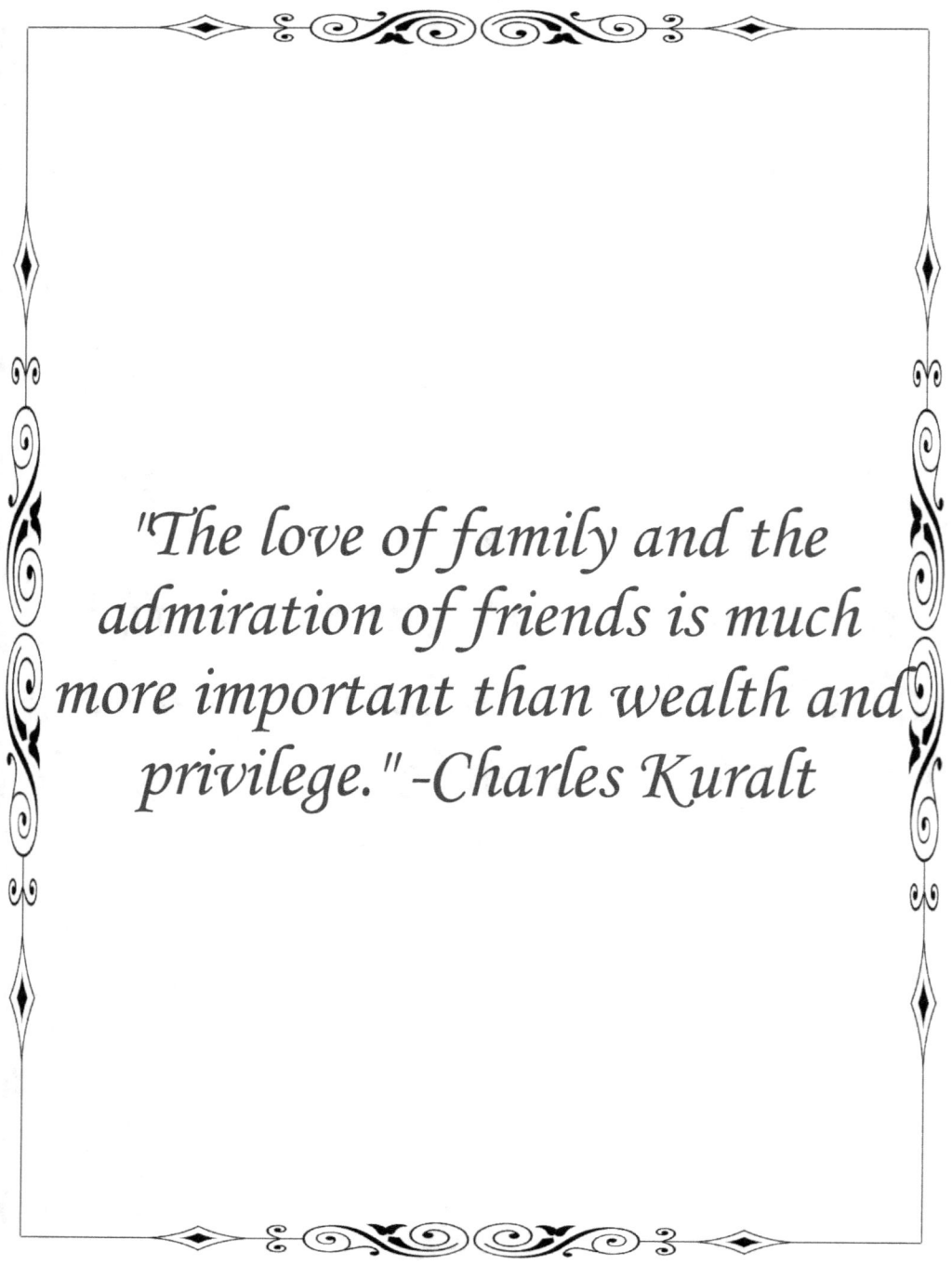

"The love of family and the admiration of friends is much more important than wealth and privilege." -Charles Kuralt

Your Daily Motivational Quote
Day 22

"Life is a journey. Enjoy the ride." -unknown

Your Daily Motivational Quote
Day 23

"Look up to the sky. You'll never find rainbows if you're looking down." -Charlie Chaplin

Your Daily Motivational Quote
Day 24

"Keep smiling because life is a beautiful thing and there is so much to smile about!" -Marilyn Monroe

Your Daily Motivational Quote
Day 25

"Don't live every day as if it were your last. Live every day as if it were your first." -Paulo Coehlo

Your Daily Motivational Quote
Day 26

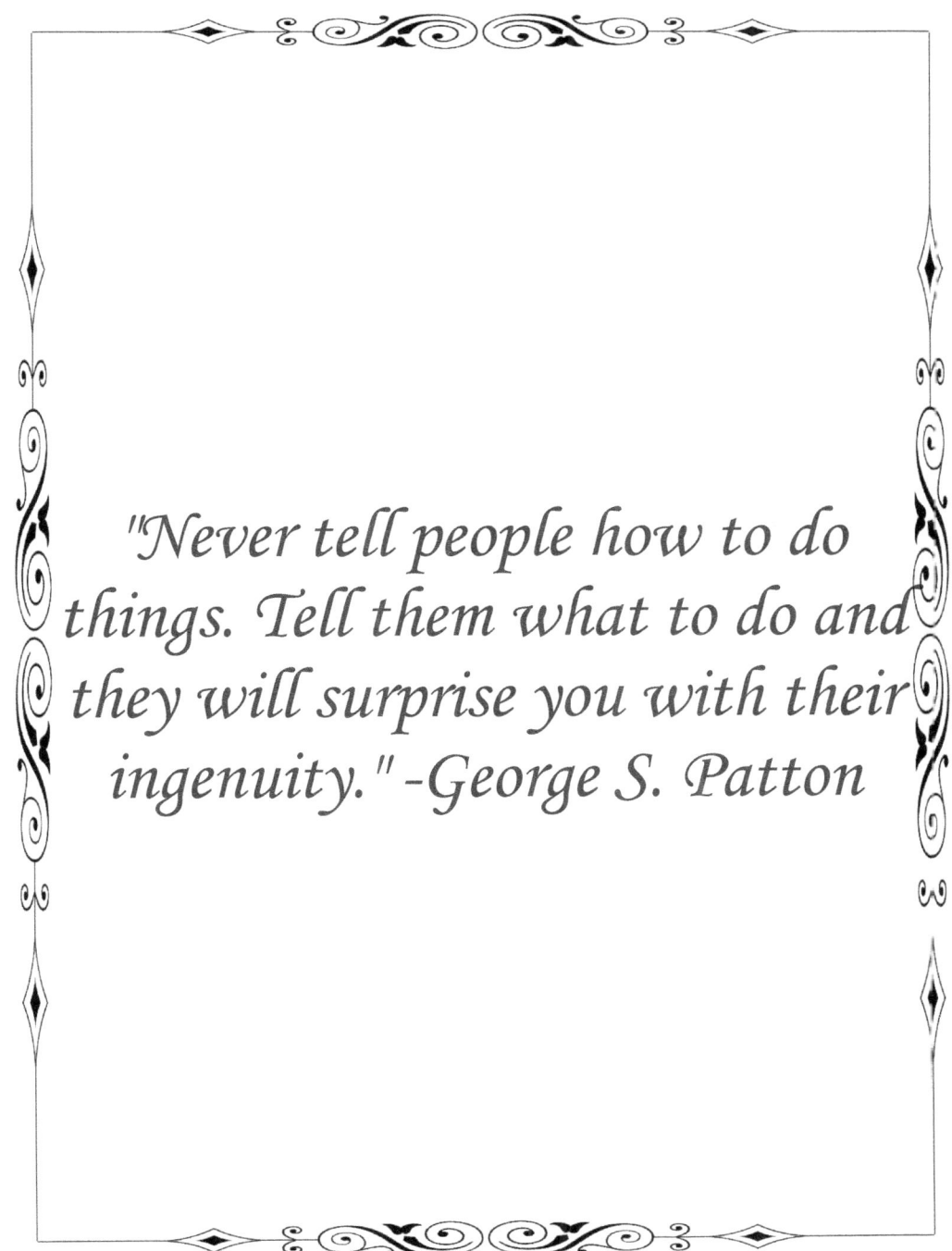

"Never tell people how to do things. Tell them what to do and they will surprise you with their ingenuity." -George S. Patton

Your Daily Motivational Quote
Day 27

"When you forgive, you in no way change the past-but you sure do change the future." - Bernard Meltzer

Your Daily Motivational Quote
Day 28

"Being honest may not get you many friends, but it'll always get you the right ones." -John Lennon

Your Daily Motivational Quote
Day 29

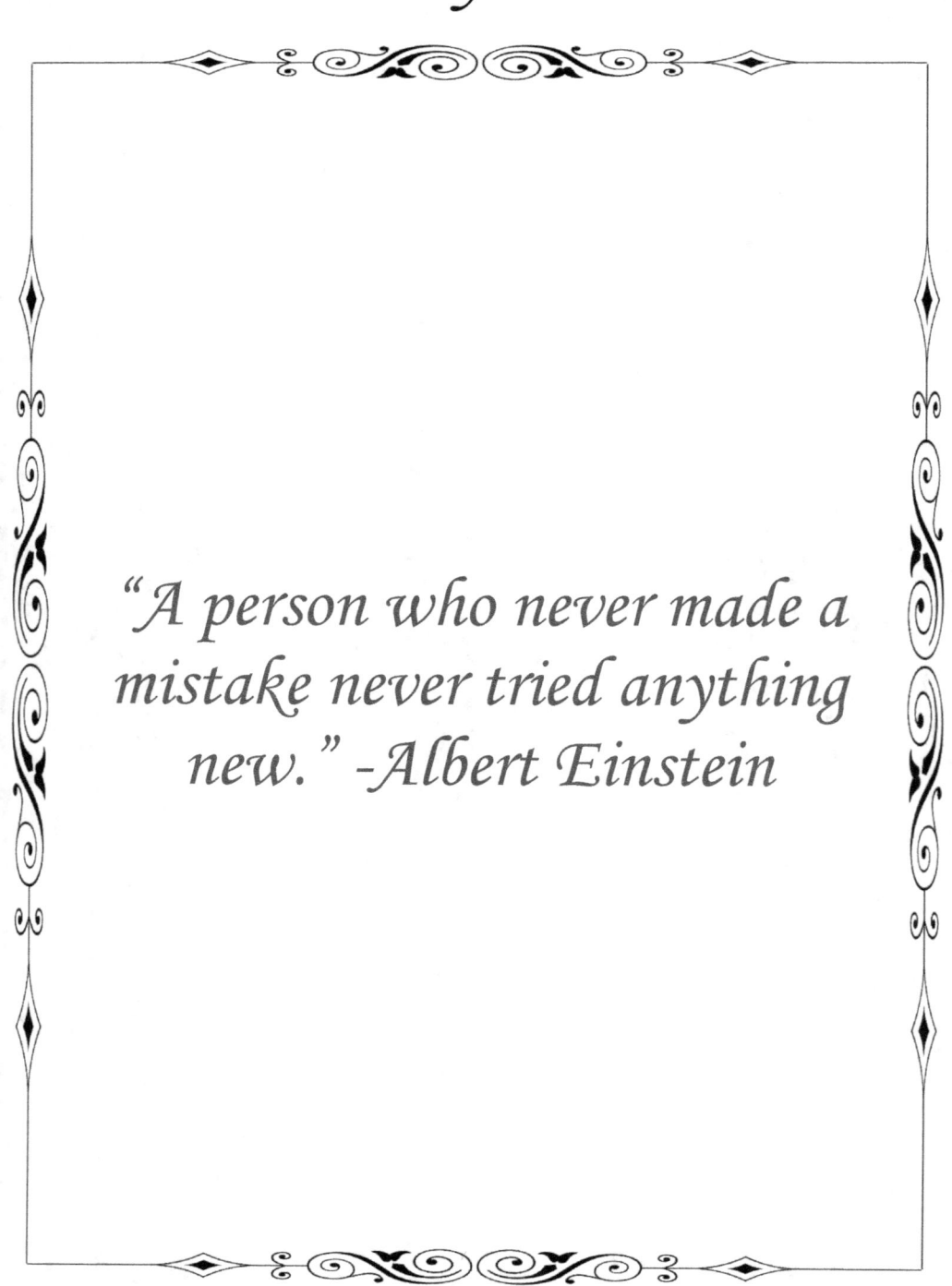

"A person who never made a mistake never tried anything new." -Albert Einstein

Your Daily Motivational Quote
Day 30

"Love is not maximum emotion. Love is maximum commitment." - Sinclair B. Ferguson

Your Daily Motivational Quote
Day 31

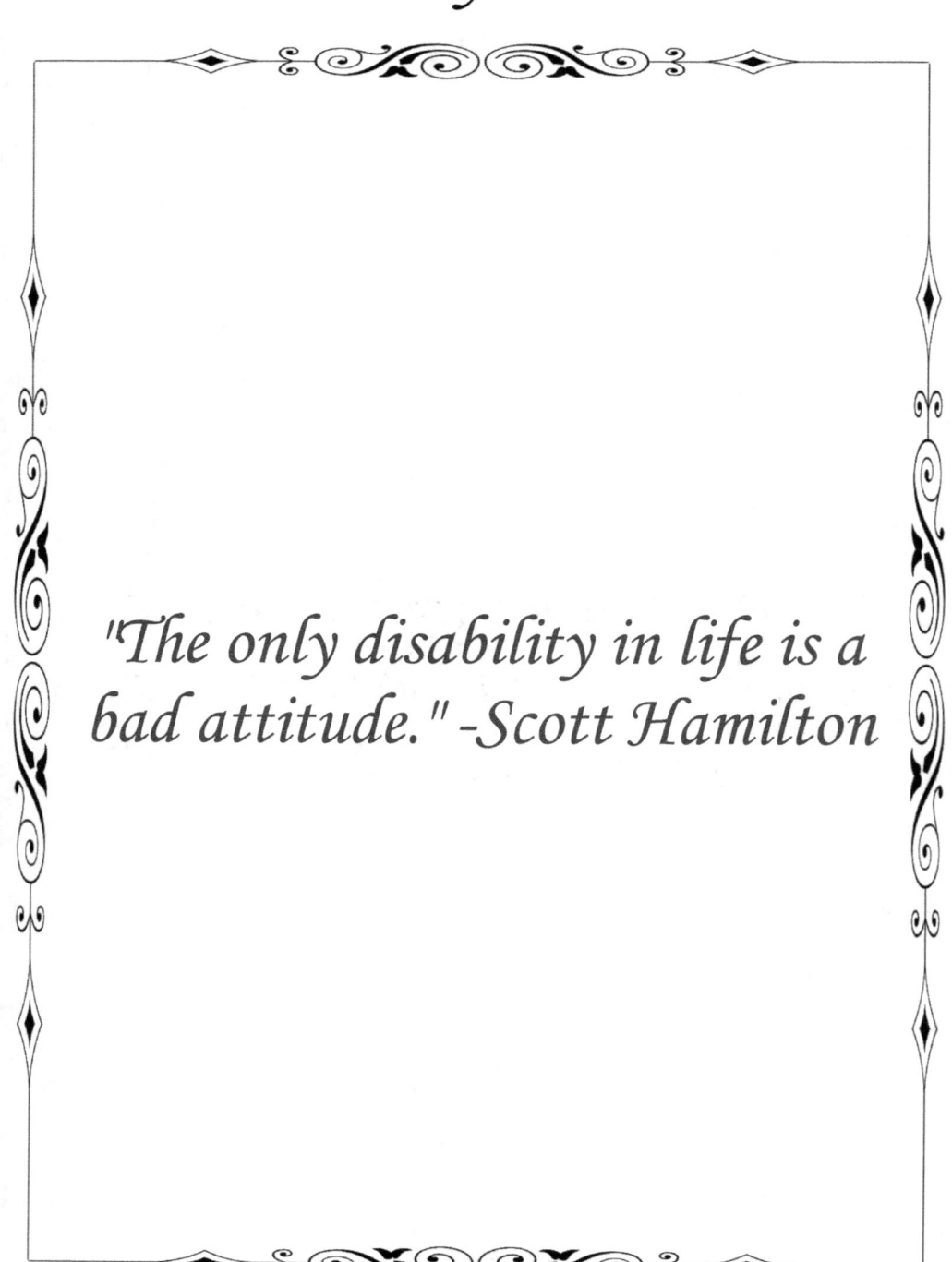

"The only disability in life is a bad attitude." -Scott Hamilton

Your Daily Motivational Quote
Day 32

"Everyone thinks of changing the world, but no one thinks of changing himself." -Leo Tolstoy

Your Daily Motivational Quote
Day 33

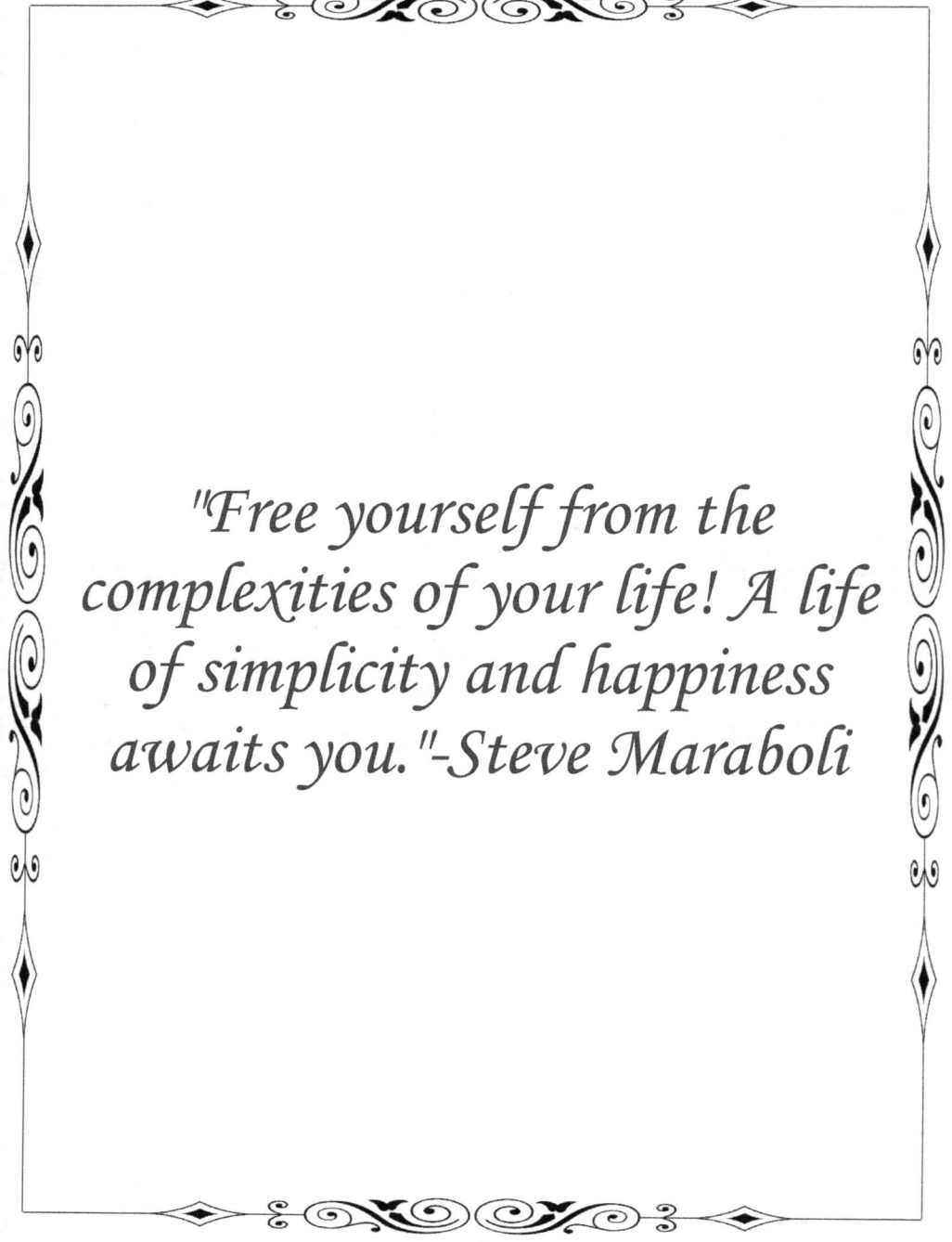

"Free yourself from the complexities of your life! A life of simplicity and happiness awaits you." -Steve Maraboli

Your Daily Motivational Quote
Day 34

"I can be a better me than anyone can." -Diana Ross

Your Daily Motivational Quote
Day 35

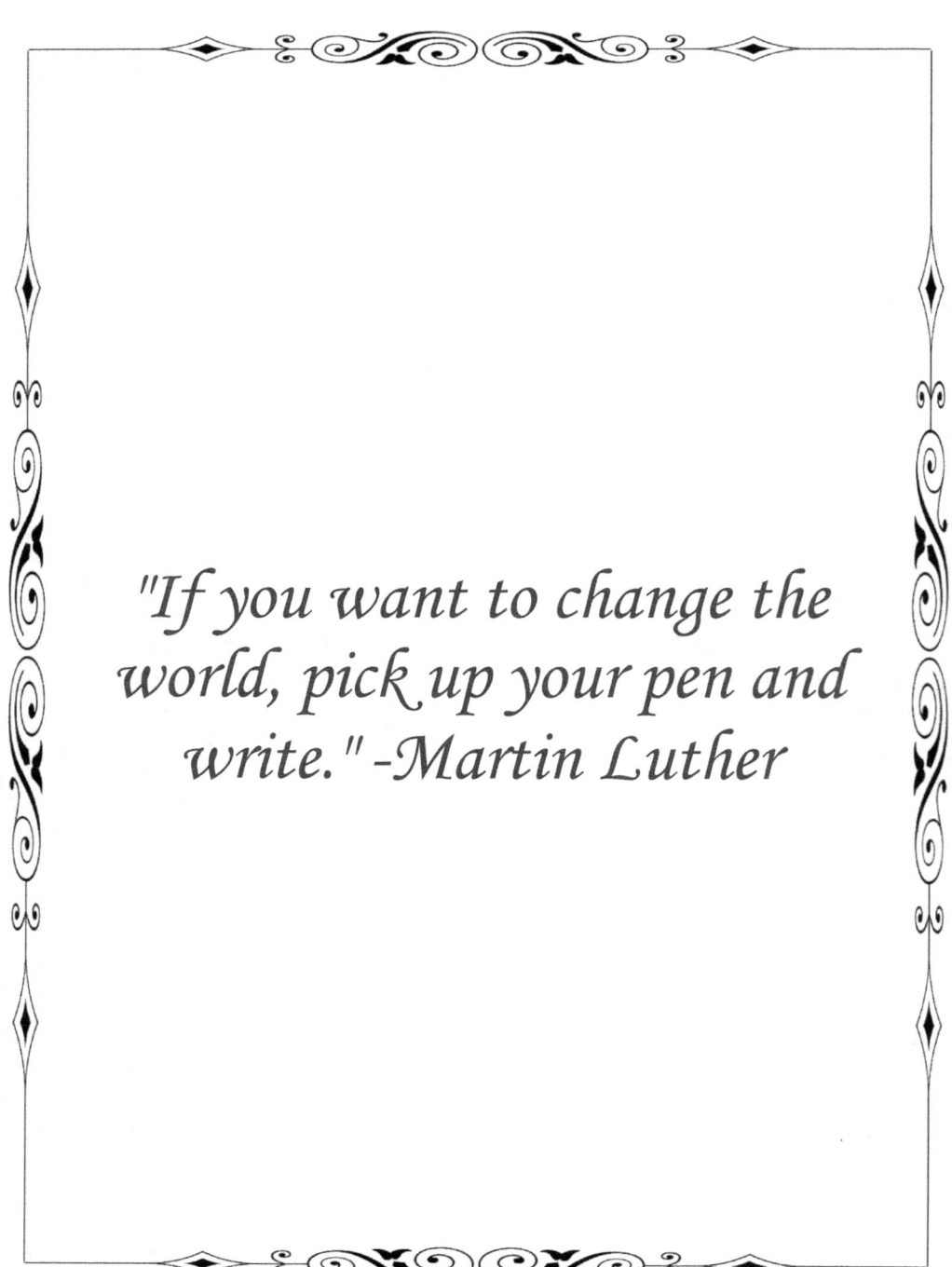

"If you want to change the world, pick up your pen and write." -Martin Luther

Your Daily Motivational Quote
Day 36

"From sun rise to shut eye, I love to celebrate life!" -unknown

Your Daily Motivational Quote
Day 37

"To laugh at yourself is to love yourself." -Mickey Mouse

Your Daily Motivational Quote
Day 38

"Intelligence without ambition is a bird without wings." -Salvador Dali

Your Daily Motivational Quote
Day 39

"Be so good they can't ignore you." -Steve Martin

Your Daily Motivational Quote
Day 40

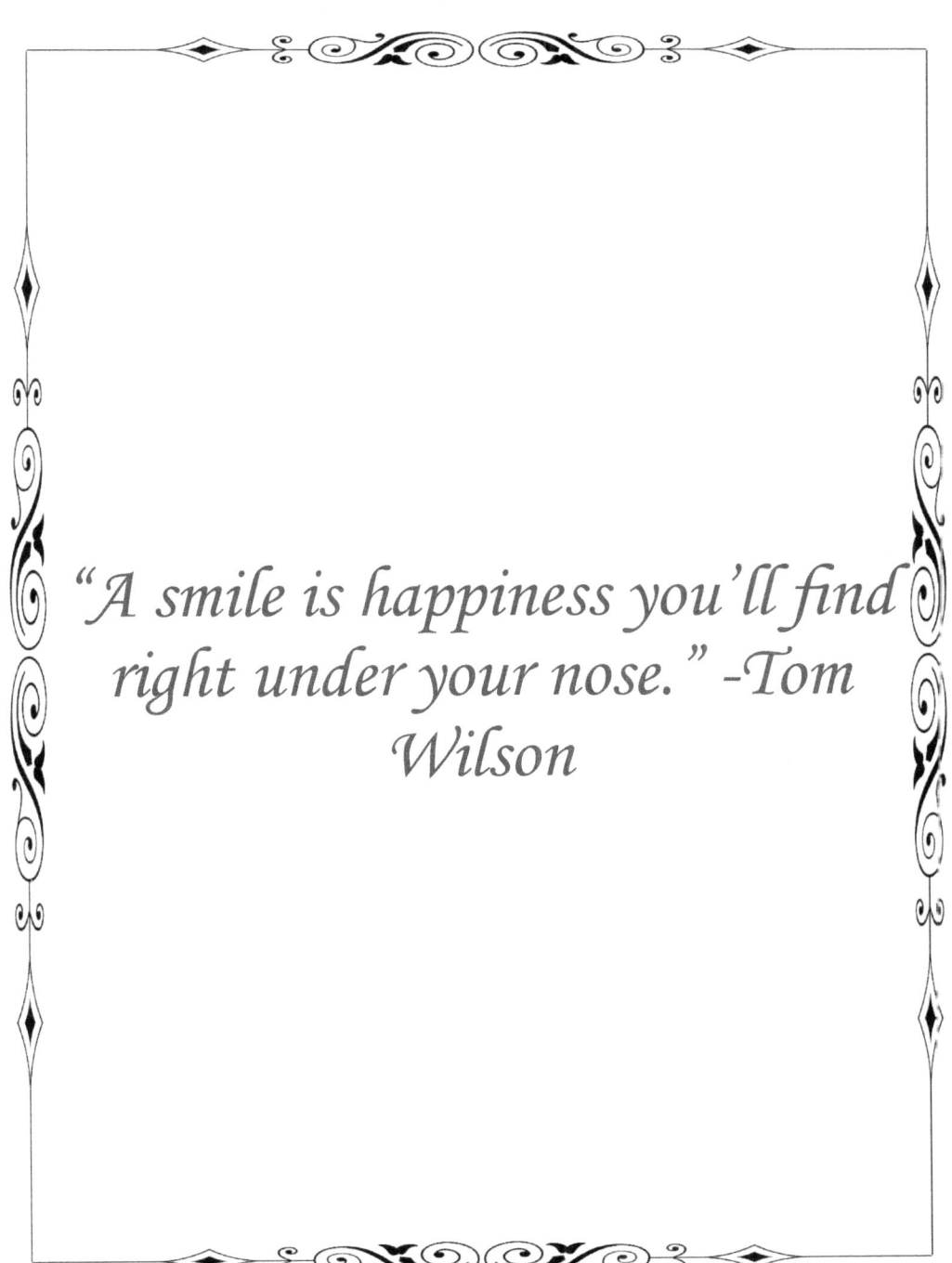

"A smile is happiness you'll find right under your nose." -Tom Wilson

Your Daily Motivational Quote
Day 41

"Yesterday is not ours to recover, but tomorrow is ours to win or lose." -Lyndon B. Johnson

Your Daily Motivational Quote
Day 42

"Life's like a movie; write your own ending." -Kermit the Frog

Your Daily Motivational Quote
Day 43

"If we are facing the right direction, all we have to do is keep on walking." -zen proverb

Your Daily Motivational Quote
Day 44

"Passion is energy. Feel the power that comes from focusing on what excites you." -Oprah Winfrey

Your Daily Motivational Quote
Day 45

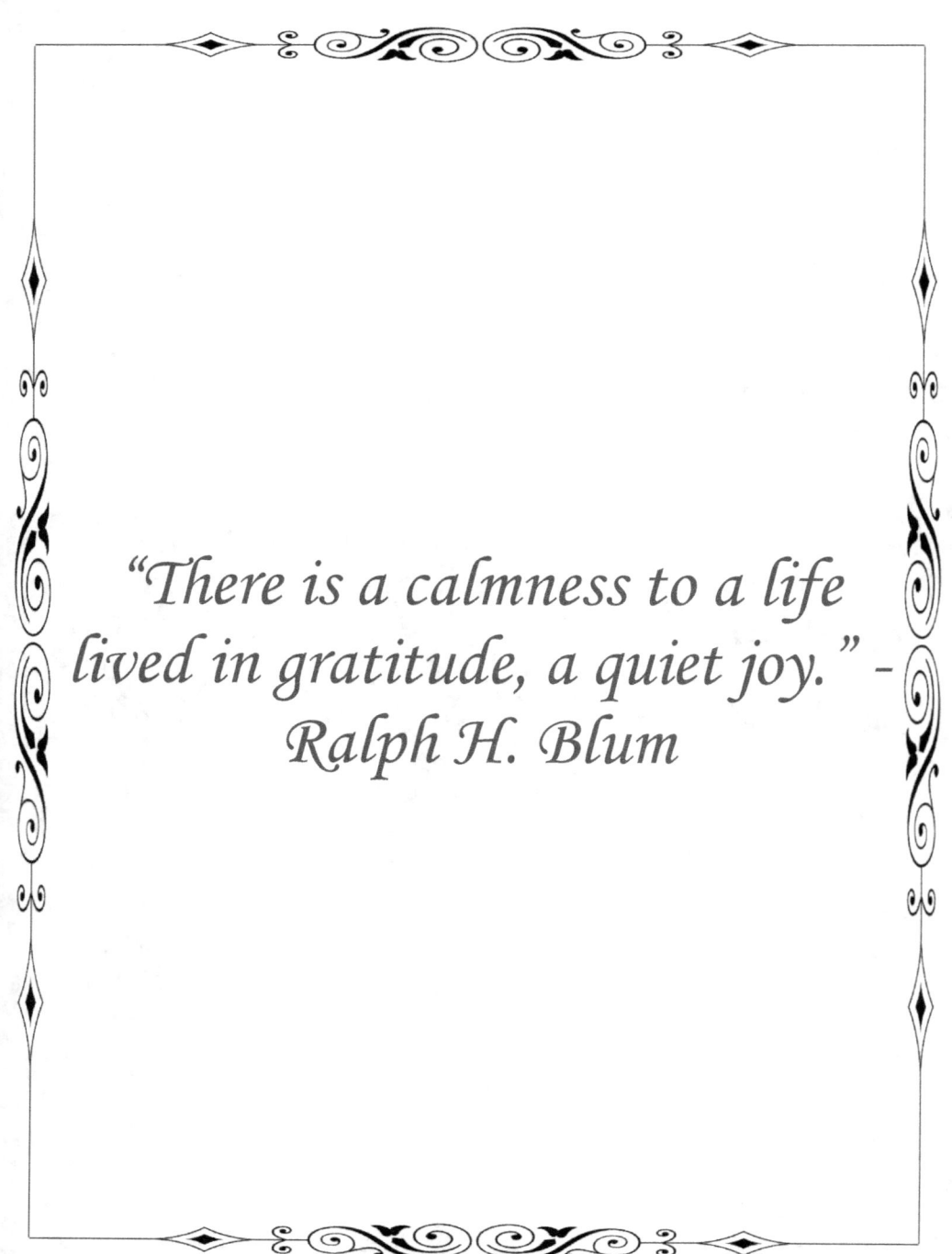

"There is a calmness to a life lived in gratitude, a quiet joy." - Ralph H. Blum

Your Daily Motivational Quote
Day 46

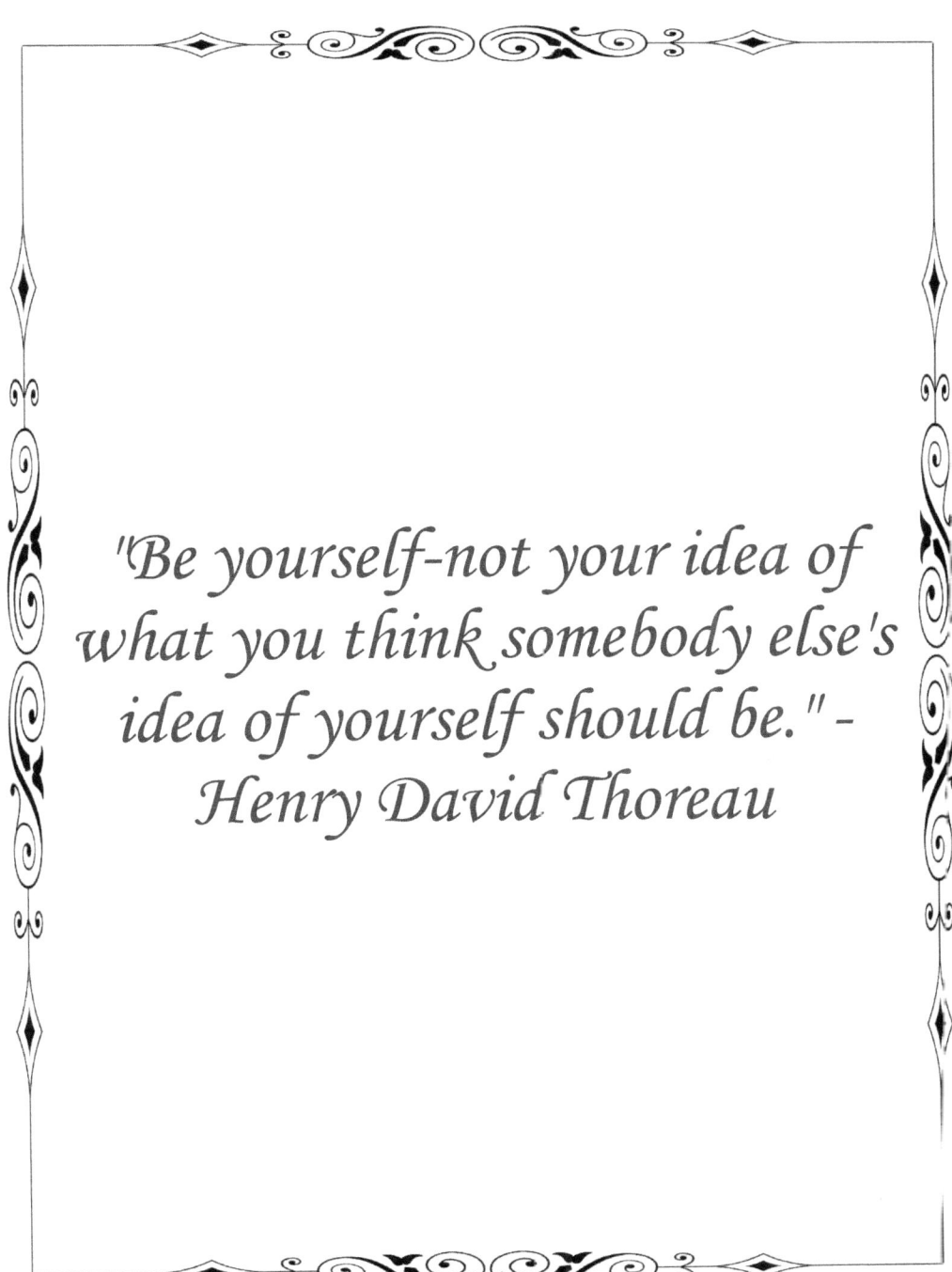

"Be yourself-not your idea of what you think somebody else's idea of yourself should be." - Henry David Thoreau

Your Daily Motivational Quote
Day 47

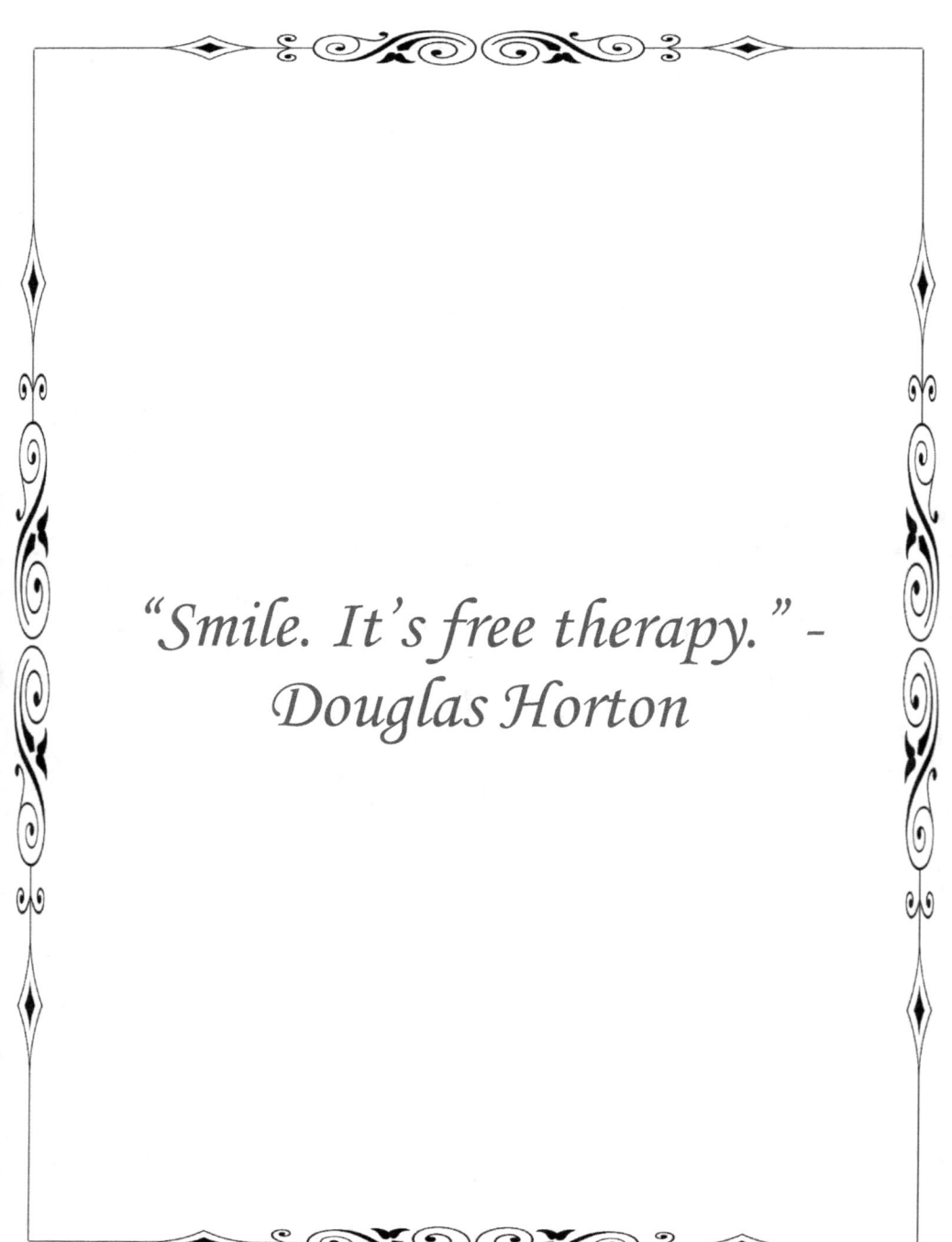

"Smile. It's free therapy." - Douglas Horton

Your Daily Motivational Quote
Day 48

"All glory comes from daring to begin." -Eugene F. Ware

Your Daily Motivational Quote
Day 49

"Seeking means: to have a goal; but finding means: to be free, to be receptive, to have no goal."- Herman Hesse

Your Daily Motivational Quote
Day 50

"Energy and persistence conquer all things." -Benjamin Franklin

Your Daily Motivational Quote
Day 51

"People who love to eat are always the best people." -Julia Child

Your Daily Motivational Quote
Day 52

"Don't quit before the miracle happens." -unknown

Your Daily Motivational Quote
Day 53

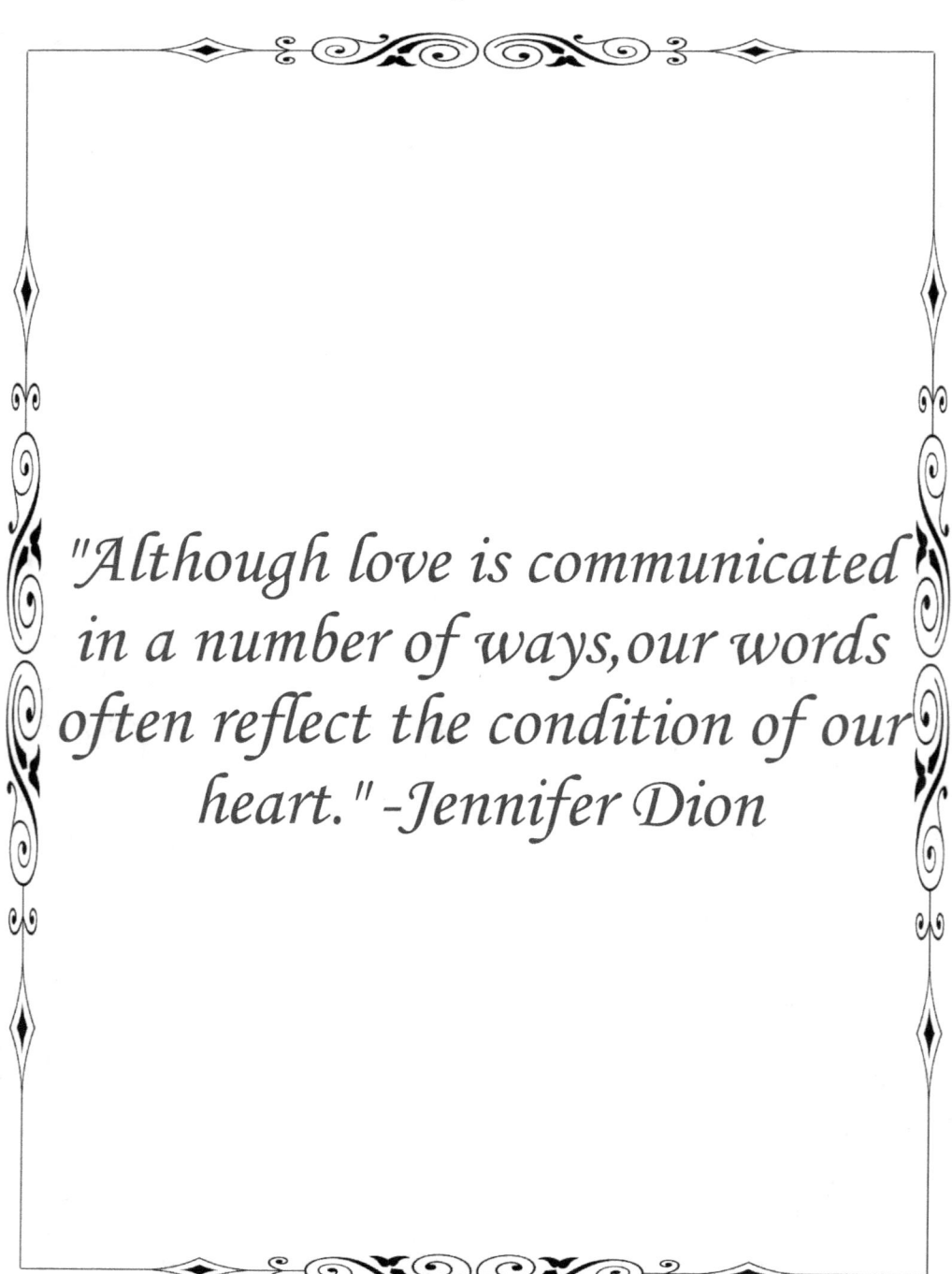

"Although love is communicated in a number of ways, our words often reflect the condition of our heart." -Jennifer Dion

Your Daily Motivational Quote
Day 54

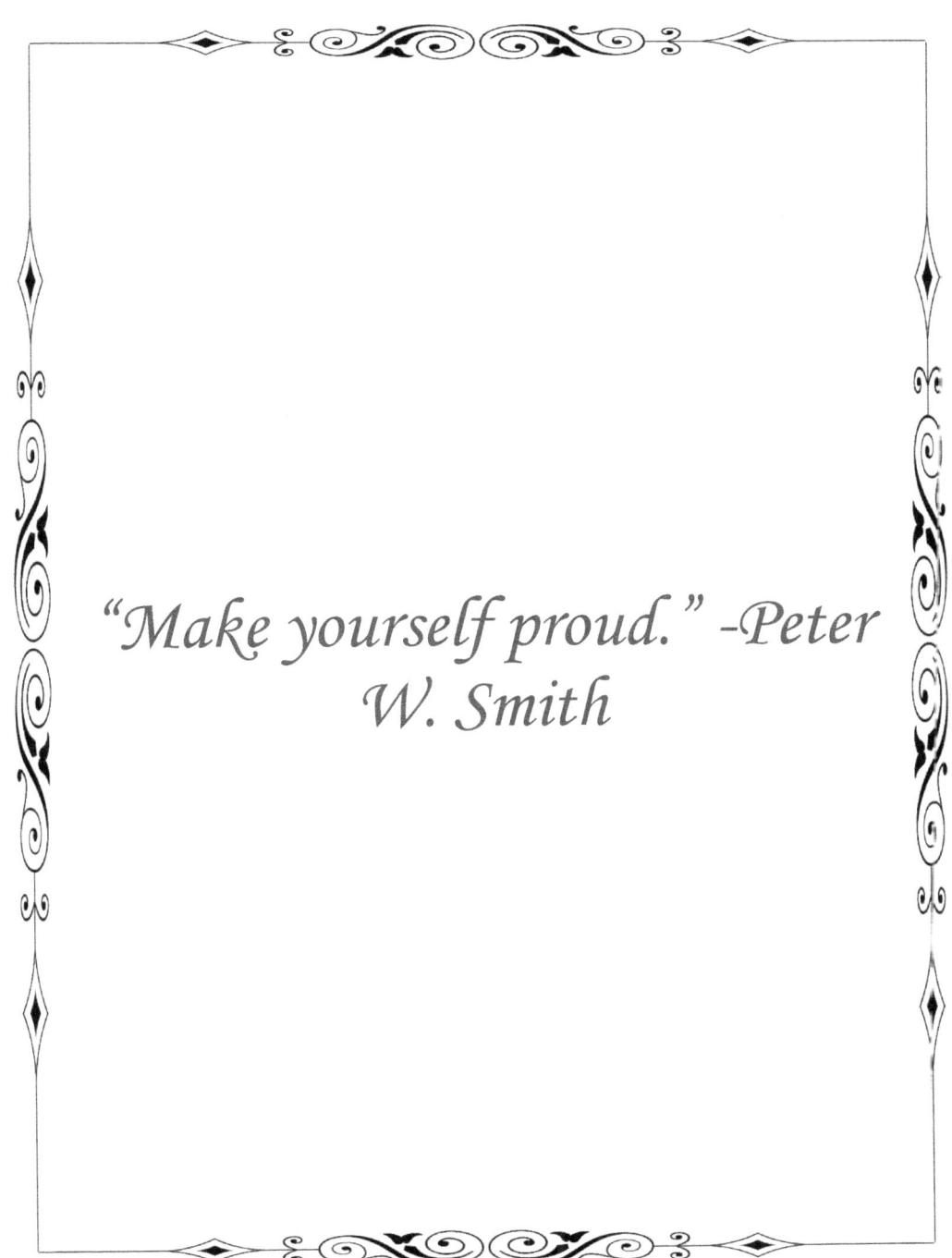

"Make yourself proud." -Peter W. Smith

Your Daily Motivational Quote
Day 55

"Those who don't believe in magic will never find it." -Roald Dahl

Your Daily Motivational Quote
Day 56

"If you can dream it you can do it." -Walt Disney

Your Daily Motivational Quote
Day 57

"Each morning when I awake, I experience again a supreme pleasure of being." -Salvador Dalí

Your Daily Motivational Quote
Day 58

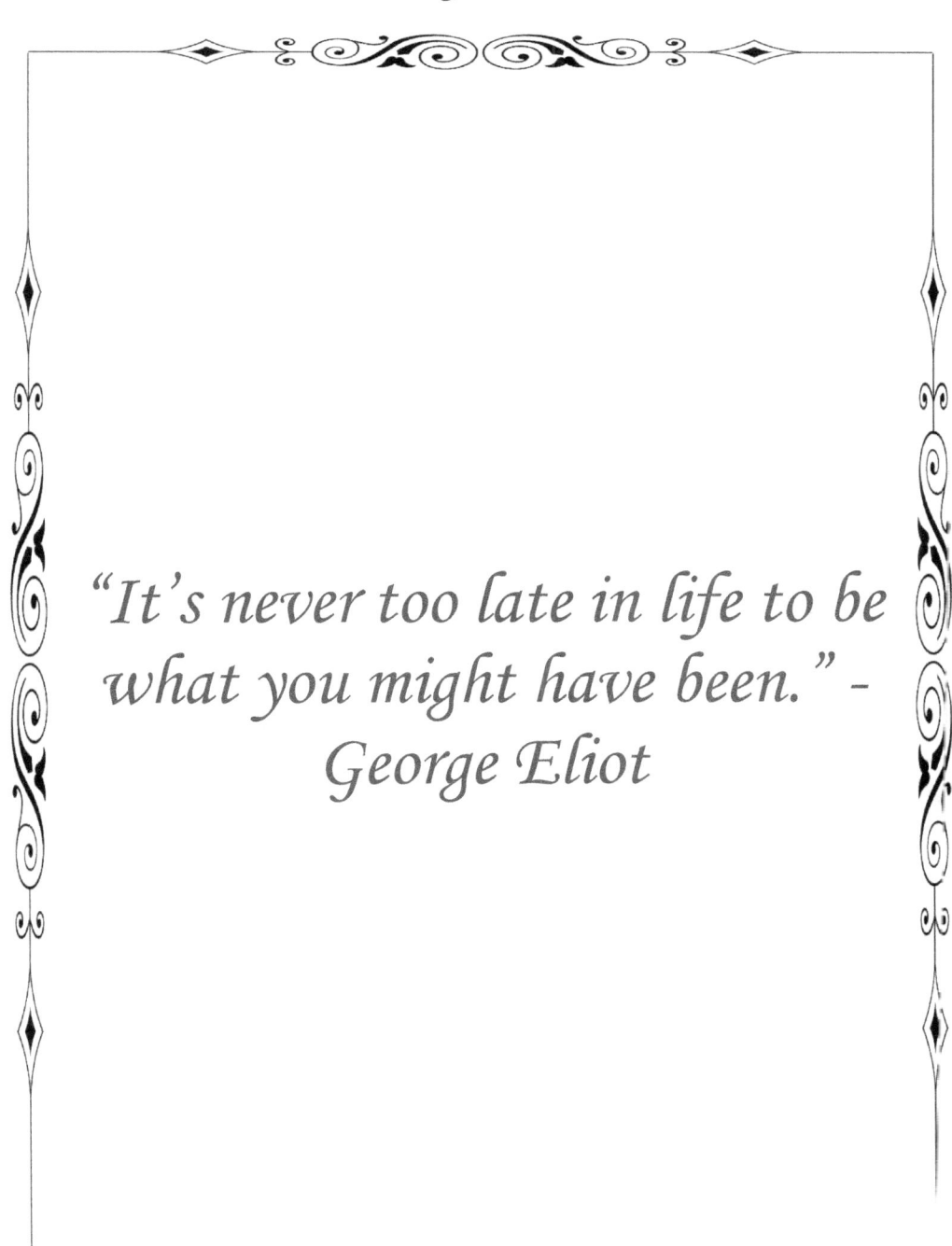

"It's never too late in life to be what you might have been." - George Eliot

Your Daily Motivational Quote
Day 59

"We must act out passion before we can feel it." -Jean-Paul Sartre

Your Daily Motivational Quote
Day 60

"Truth is so rare that it is delightful to tell it." -Emily Dickinson

Your Daily Motivational Quote
Day 61

"Simplicity is the ultimate sophistication." -Leonardo da Vinci

Your Daily Motivational Quote
Day 62

"Life is an adventure! So live it up!" -L.M. Preston

Your Daily Motivational Quote
Day 63

"The best is yet to be." -Robert Browning

Your Daily Motivational Quote
Day 64

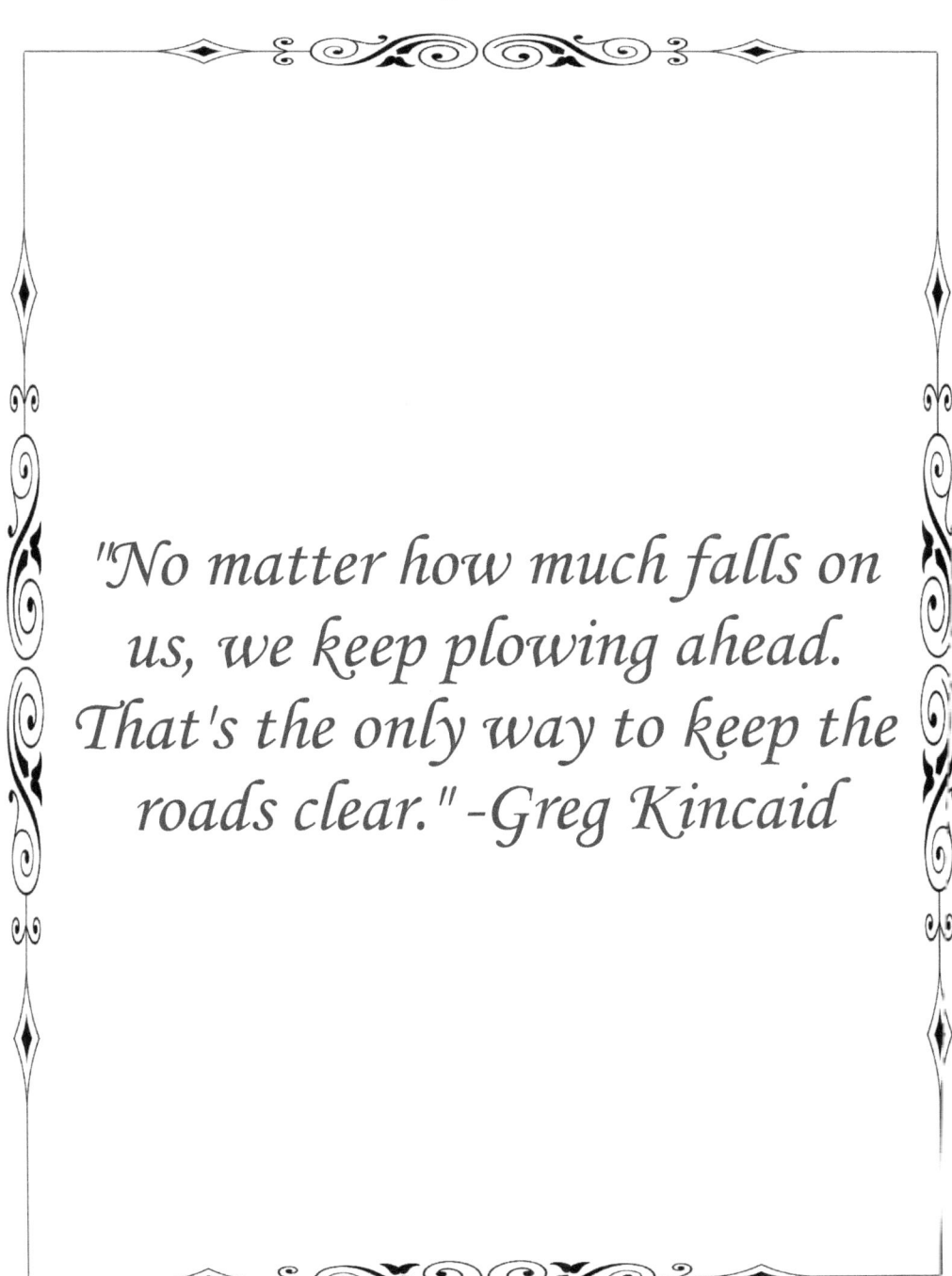

"No matter how much falls on us, we keep plowing ahead. That's the only way to keep the roads clear." -Greg Kincaid

Your Daily Motivational Quote
Day 65

"Friendship isn't a big thing; it's a million little things." - anonymous

Your Daily Motivational Quote
Day 66

"Life begins at the end of your comfort zone." -Neale Donald Walsch

Your Daily Motivational Quote
Day 67

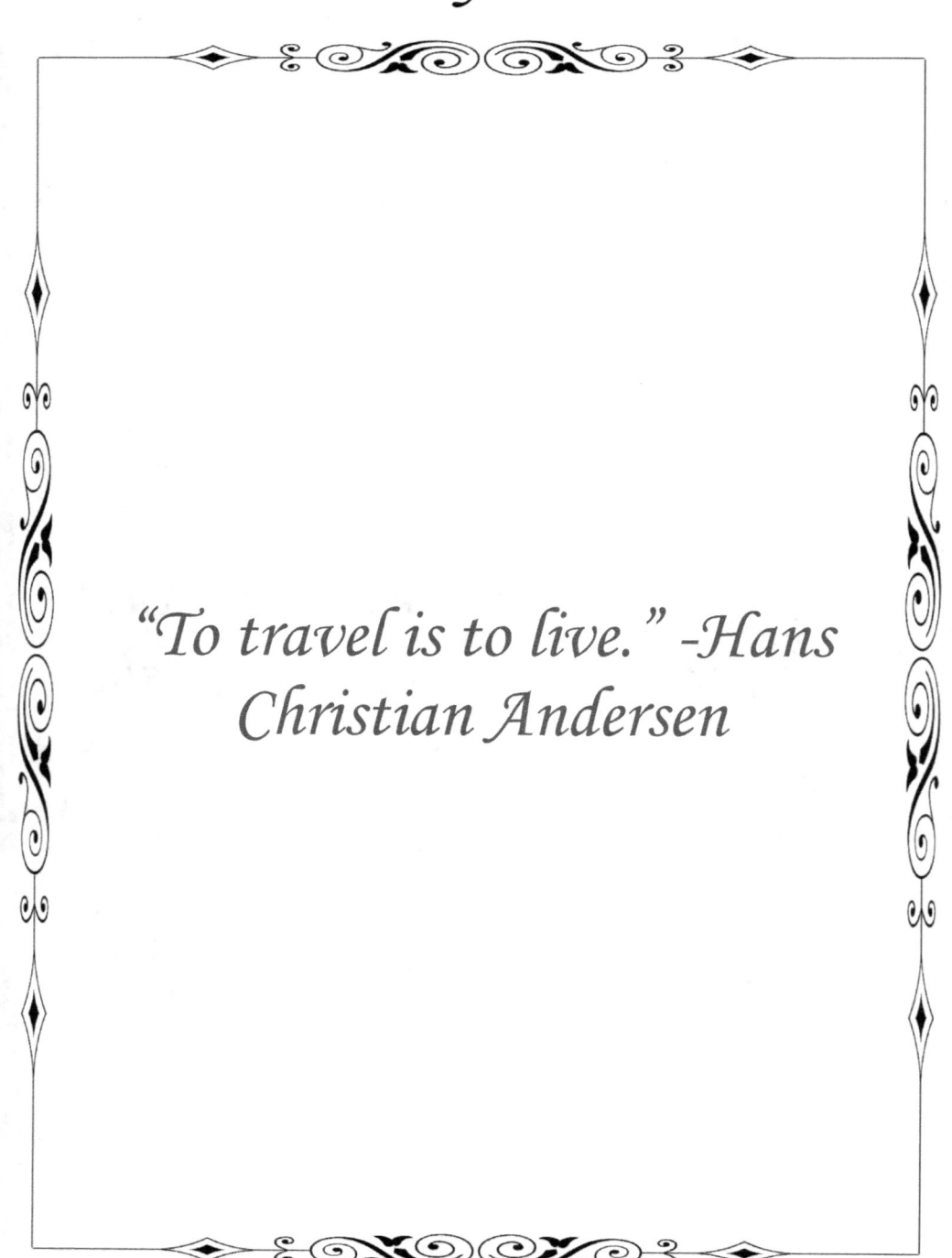

"To travel is to live." -Hans Christian Andersen

Your Daily Motivational Quote
Day 68

"Beauty is being the best possible version of yourself, inside and out." -Audrey Hepburn

Your Daily Motivational Quote
Day 69

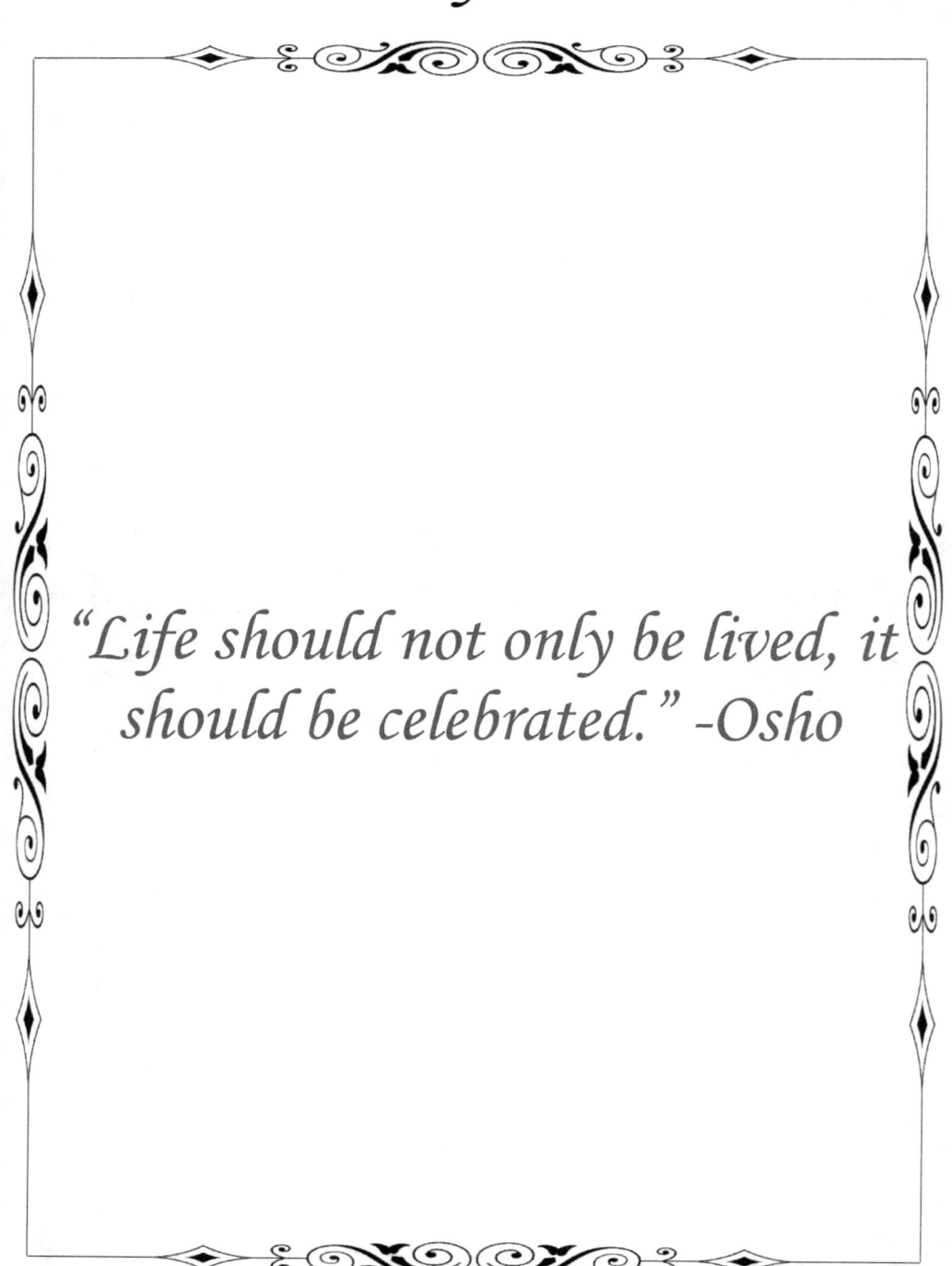

"Life should not only be lived, it should be celebrated." -Osho

Your Daily Motivational Quote
Day 70

"Enjoy the little things in life… for one day you'll look back and realize that they were big things." -Robert Brault

Your Daily Motivational Quote
Day 71

"Sunsets are proof that no matter what happens, every day can end beautifully." -Kristin Butler

Your Daily Motivational Quote
Day 72

"The keys to brand success are self-definition, transparency, authenticity and accountability."
-Simon Mainwaring

Your Daily Motivational Quote
Day 73

"There is no passion to be found playing small-in settling for a life that is less than the one you are capable of living." -Nelson Mandela

Your Daily Motivational Quote
Day 74

"Eyes so transparent that through them the soul is seen." - Theophile Gautier

Your Daily Motivational Quote
Day 75

"Talent wins games, but teamwork and intelligence wins championships." -Michael Jordan

Your Daily Motivational Quote
Day 76

"Beauty begins the moment you decide to be yourself." -Coco Chanel

Your Daily Motivational Quote
Day 77

"When you're happy, you find pure joy in your life. There are no regrets in this state of happiness – and that's a goal worth striving for in all areas of your life." -Suze Orman

Your Daily Motivational Quote
Day 78

"Keep love in your heart. A life without it is like a sunless garden when the flowers are dead." -Oscar Wilde

Your Daily Motivational Quote
Day 79

"There is no end. There is no beginning. There is only the passion of life. There is no end. There is no beginning. There is only the passion of life." - Federico Fellini

Your Daily Motivational Quote
Day 80

"Truth never damages a cause that is just." -Mahatma Gandhi

Your Daily Motivational Quote
Day 81

"Authenticity requires a certain measure of vulnerability, transparency, and integrity" - Janet Louise Stepenson

Your Daily Motivational Quote
Day 82

"Don't tell me the sky is the limit when there are footprints on the moon." -Paul Brandt

Your Daily Motivational Quote
Day 83

"Be happy for this moment. This moment is your life." -Omar Khayyam

Your Daily Motivational Quote
Day 84

"The art of life is a constant readjustment to our surroundings." -Kakuzo Okakaura

Your Daily Motivational Quote
Day 85

"If passion drives you, let reason hold the reins." -Benjamin Franklin

Your Daily Motivational Quote
Day 86

"Just catch the wind and go." - Heather Maloney

Your Daily Motivational Quote
Day 87

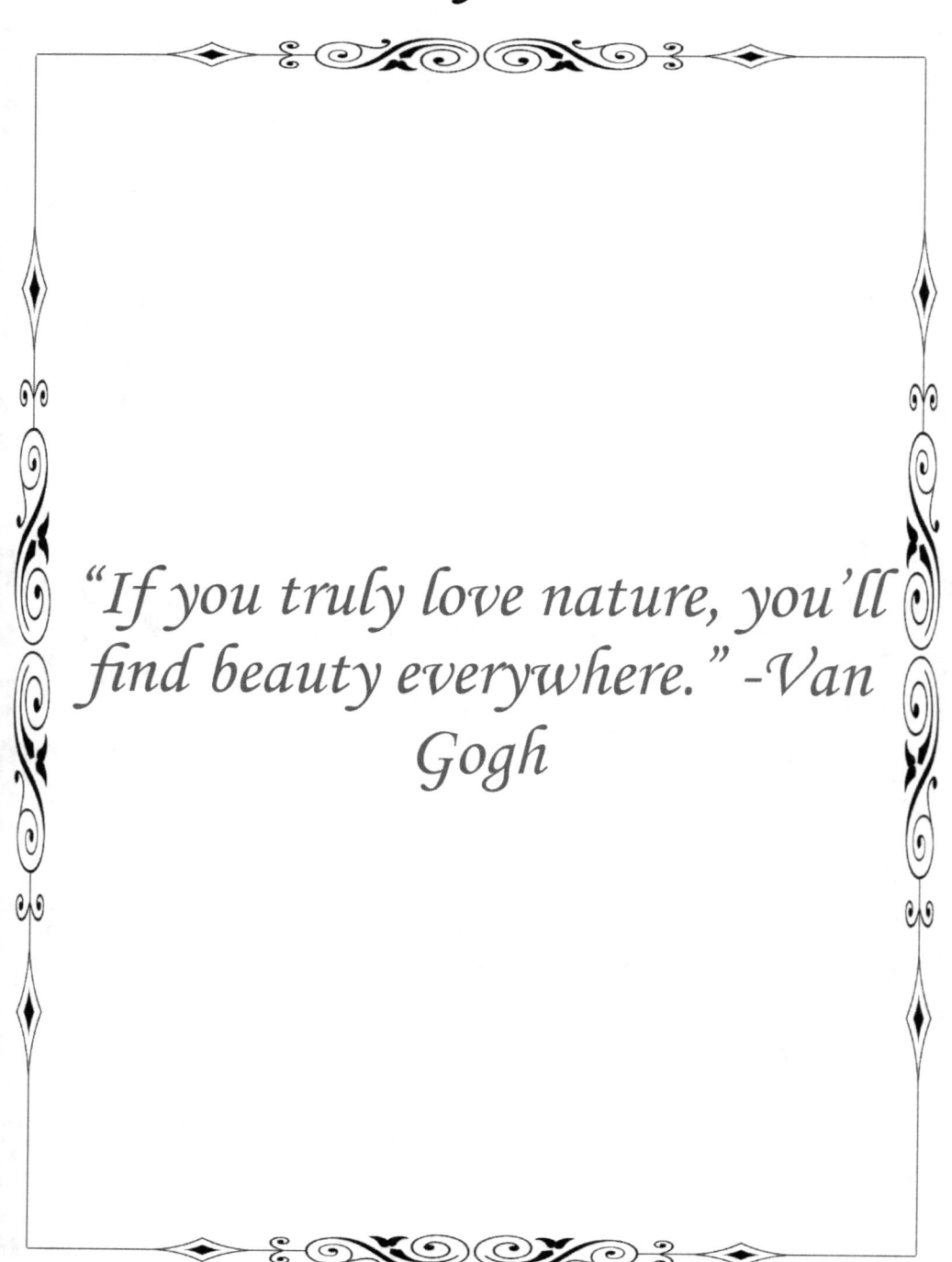

"If you truly love nature, you'll find beauty everywhere." -Van Gogh

Your Daily Motivational Quote
Day 88

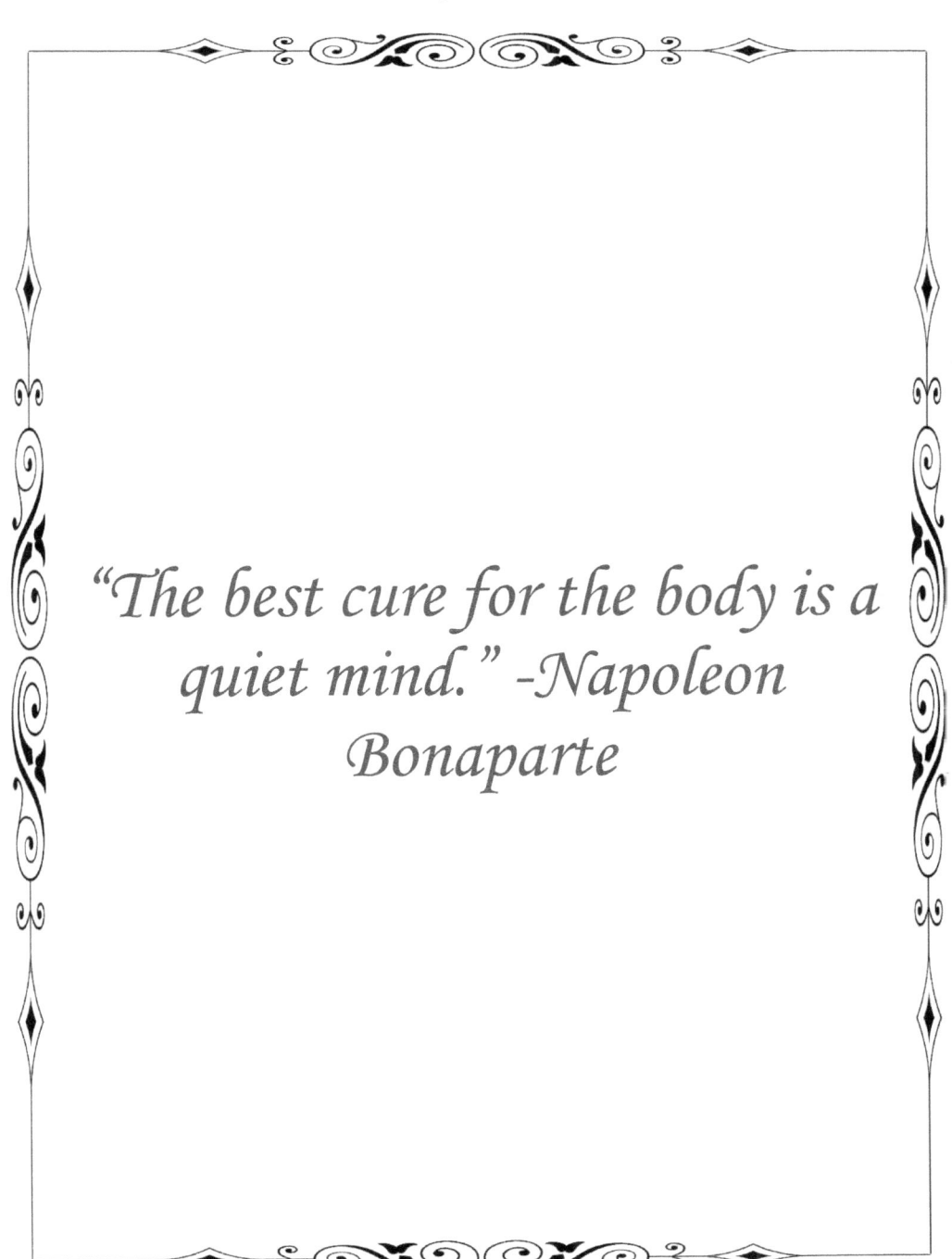

"The best cure for the body is a quiet mind." -Napoleon Bonaparte

Your Daily Motivational Quote
Day 89

"Don't find a fault, find a remedy." -Henry Ford

Your Daily Motivational Quote
Day 90

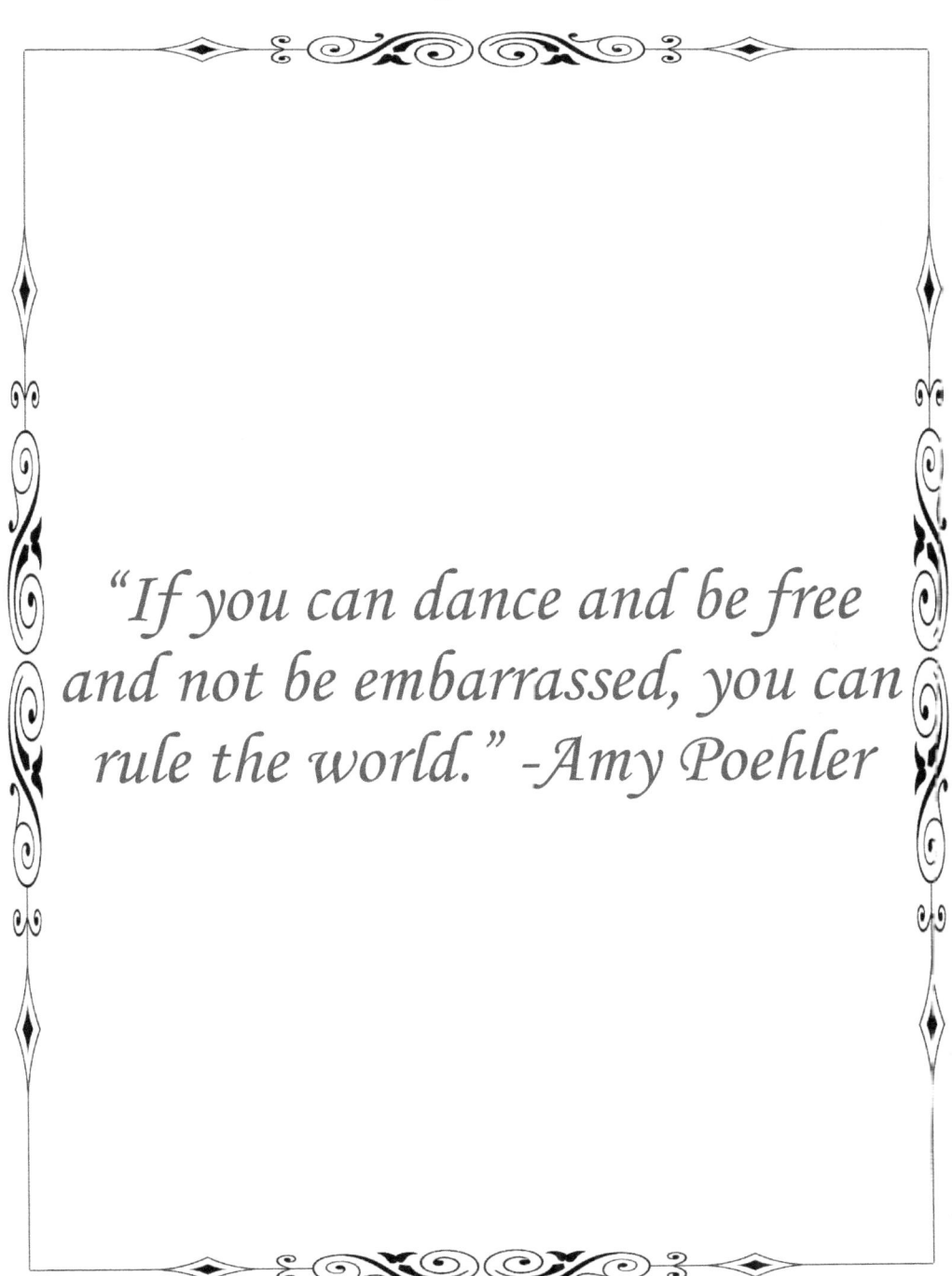

"If you can dance and be free and not be embarrassed, you can rule the world." -Amy Poehler

Your Daily Motivational Quote
Day 91

"Let us always meet each other with smile, for the smile is the beginning of love." -Mother Teresa

Your Daily Motivational Quote
Day 92

"First keep peace with yourself, then you can also bring peace to others." -Thomas Kempis

Your Daily Motivational Quote
Day 93

"The beautiful journey of today can only begin when we learn to let go of yesterday." -Steve Maraboli

Your Daily Motivational Quote
Day 94

"The proud man can learn humility, but he will be proud of it." -Mignon McLaughlin

Your Daily Motivational Quote
Day 95

"Change is the end result of all true learning." -Leo Buscaglia

Your Daily Motivational Quote
Day 96

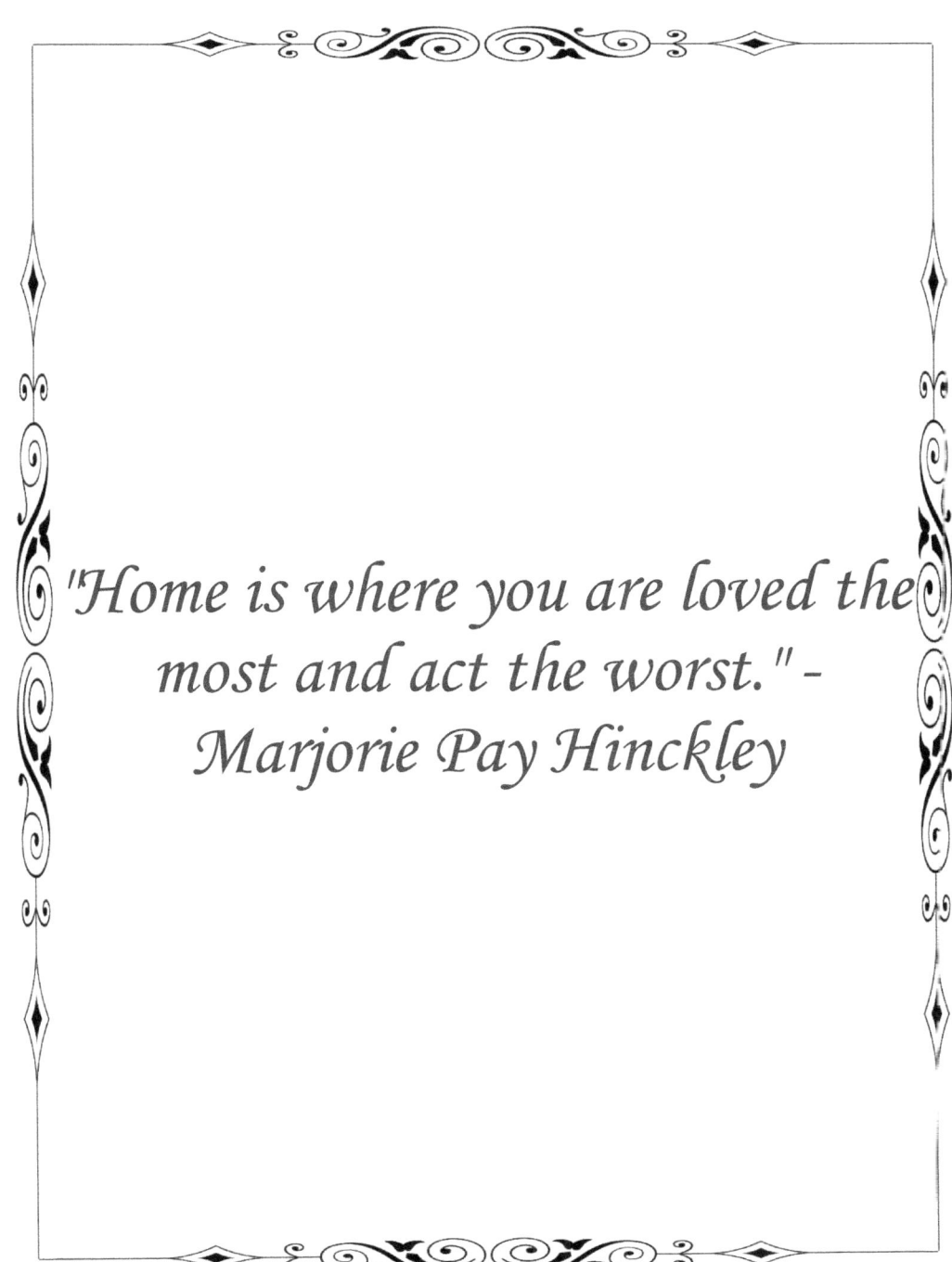

"Home is where you are loved the most and act the worst." - Marjorie Pay Hinckley

Your Daily Motivational Quote
Day 97

"Life is a succession of lessons which must be lived to be understood." -Helen Keller

Your Daily Motivational Quote
Day 98

"Discovery consists not in seeking new lands but in seeing with new eyes." -Marcel Proust

Your Daily Motivational Quote
Day 99

"It's the little things that make life wonderful." -unknown

Your Daily Motivational Quote
Day 100

"Just living is not enough… One must have sunshine, freedom, and a little flower." -Hans Christine Andersen

Your Daily Motivational Quote
Day 101

"Today is the start of a new adventure. New challenges to face, new memories to make, and new obstacles to overcome." - Nishan Panwar

Your Daily Motivational Quote
Day 102

"Let your soul stand cool and composed before a million universes." -Walt Whitman

Your Daily Motivational Quote
Day 103

"We must find time to stop and thank the people who make a difference in our lives." -John F. Kennedy

Your Daily Motivational Quote
Day 104

"Friendship is when people know all about you but love you anyway." -anonymous

Your Daily Motivational Quote
Day 105

"If you haven't done much giving in your life-try it and see how you feel afterwards." -Michelle Moore

Your Daily Motivational Quote
Day 106

"If you haven't found it yet, keep looking." -Steve Jobs

Your Daily Motivational Quote
Day 107

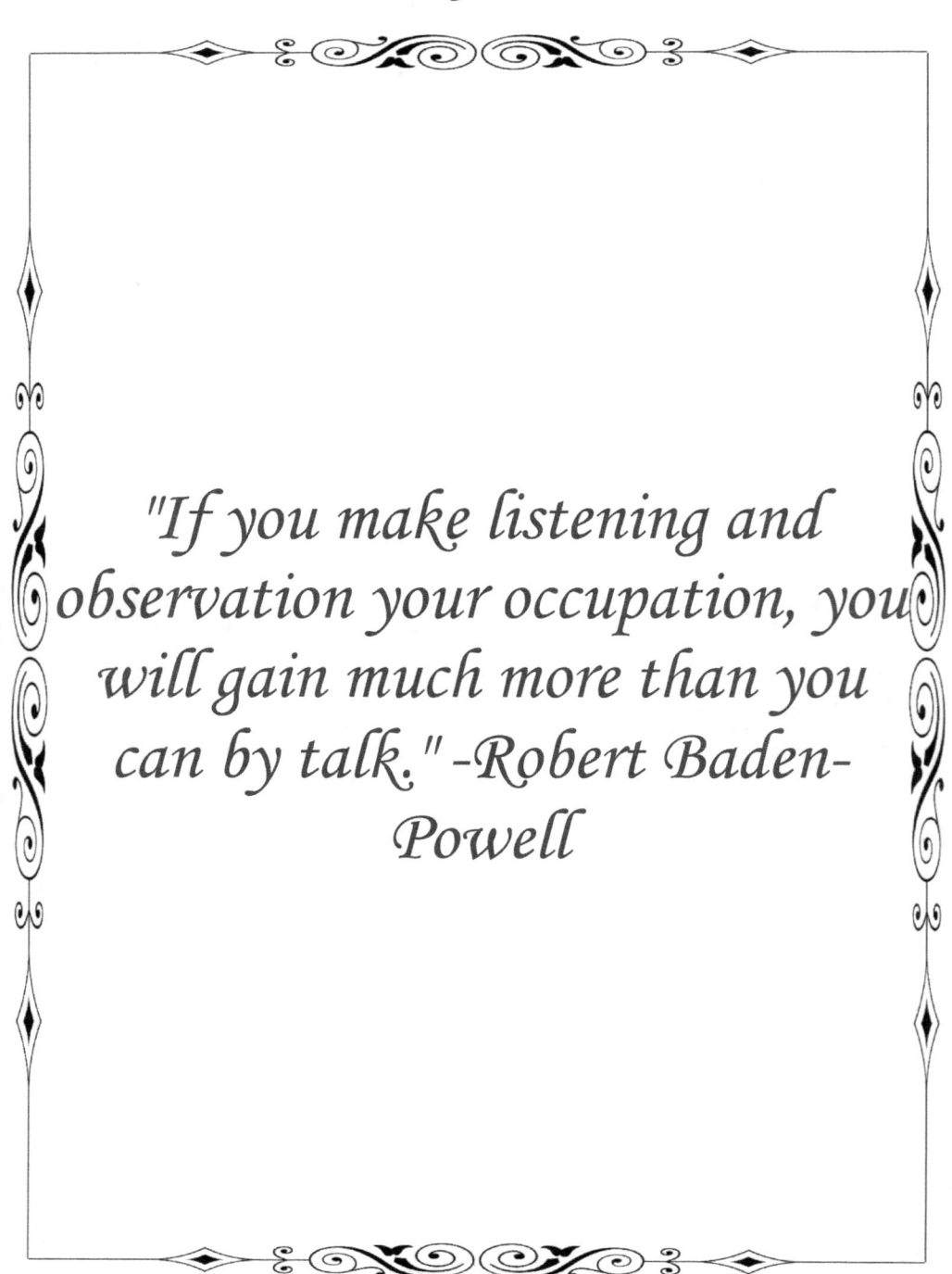

"If you make listening and observation your occupation, you will gain much more than you can by talk." -Robert Baden-Powell

Your Daily Motivational Quote
Day 108

"You feel your strength in the experience of pain." -Jim Morrison

Your Daily Motivational Quote
Day 109

"A loving heart is the beginning of all knowledge." -Thomas Carlyle

Your Daily Motivational Quote
Day 110

"Confidence, like art, never comes from having all the answers; it comes from being open to all the questions." -Earl Gray Stevens

Your Daily Motivational Quote
Day 111

"Adaptability is not imitation. It means power of resistance and assimilation." -Mahatma Gandhi

Your Daily Motivational Quote
Day 112

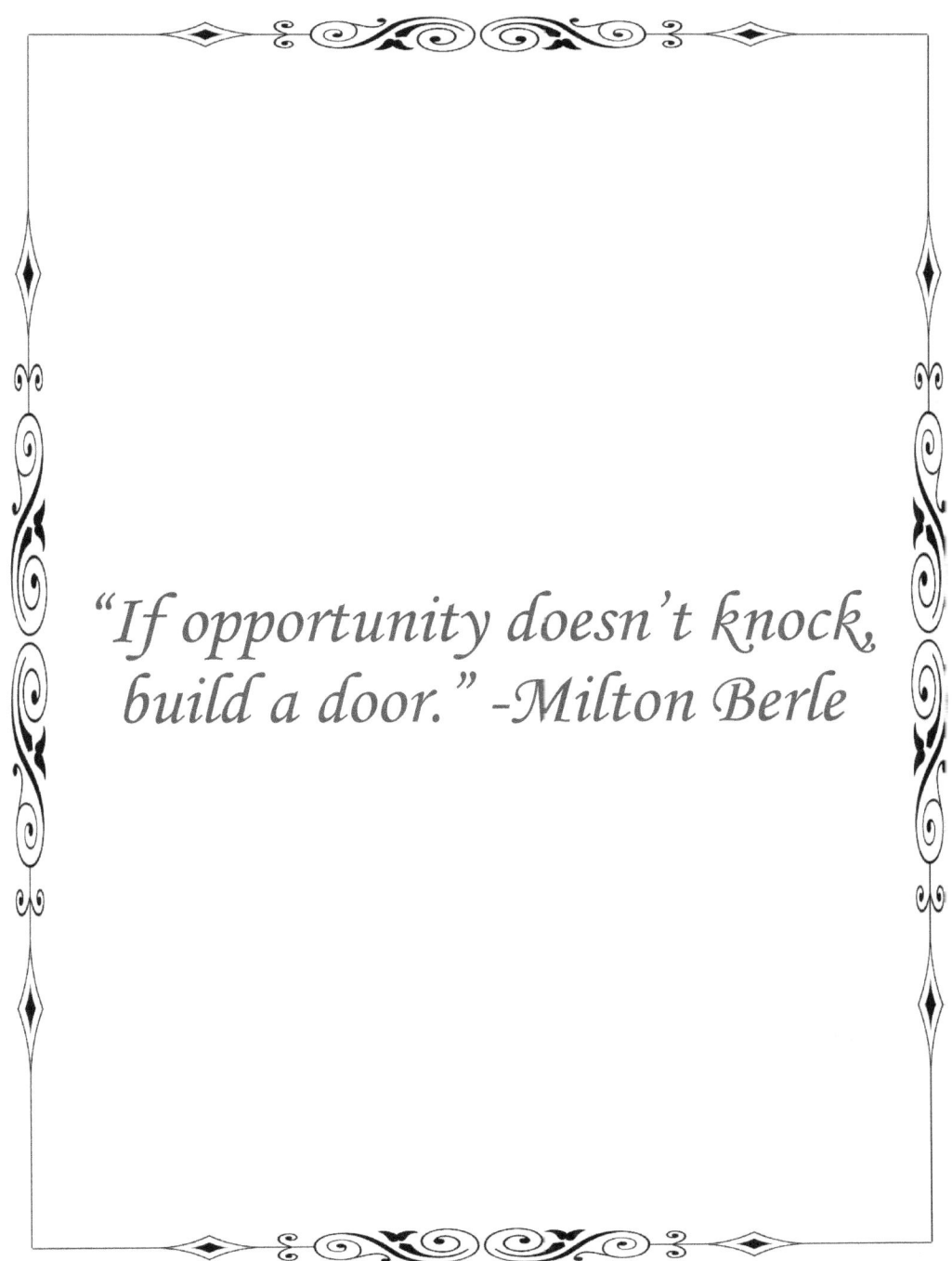

"If opportunity doesn't knock, build a door." -Milton Berle

Your Daily Motivational Quote
Day 113

"Explore the crazy, embrace the wild." -Lisa Messenger

Your Daily Motivational Quote
Day 114

"There is no love without forgiveness, and there is no forgiveness without love." - Bryant H. McGill

Your Daily Motivational Quote
Day 115

"Family means no one gets left behind or forgotten." -David Ogden Stiers

Your Daily Motivational Quote
Day 116

"Its not always necessary to be strong, but to feel strong." -Jon Krakauer

Your Daily Motivational Quote
Day 117

"With the new day comes new strength and new thoughts." - Eleanor Roosevelt

Your Daily Motivational Quote
Day 118

"The things you do for yourself are gone when you are gone, but the things you do for others remain as your legacy." -Kalu Ndukwe Kalu

Your Daily Motivational Quote
Day 119

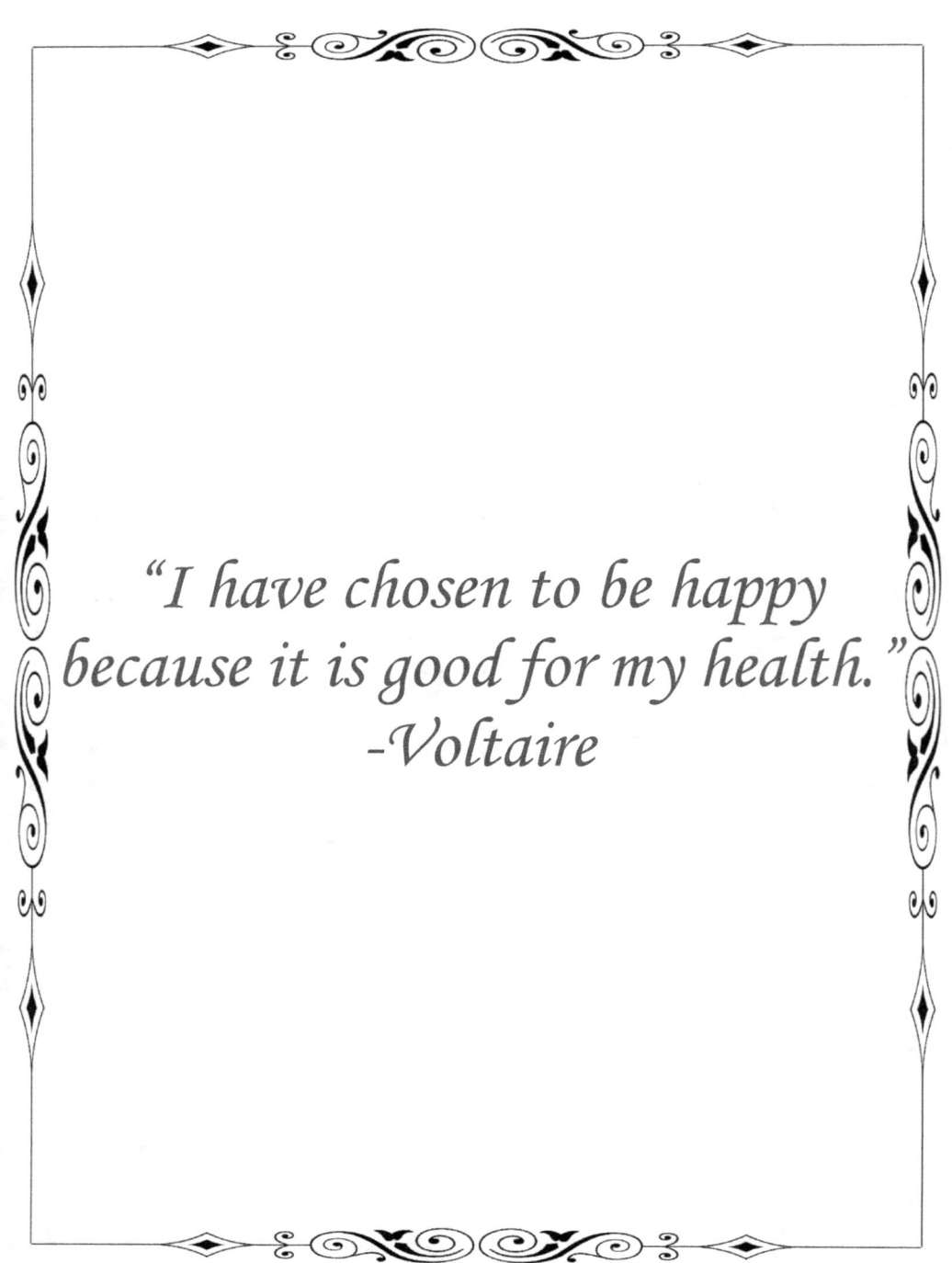

"*I have chosen to be happy because it is good for my health.*"
-Voltaire

Your Daily Motivational Quote
Day 120

"They always say time changes things, but you actually have to change them yourself." -Andy Warhol

Your Daily Motivational Quote
Day 121

"Logic will get you from A to B. Imagination will take you everywhere." -Albert Einstein

Your Daily Motivational Quote
Day 122

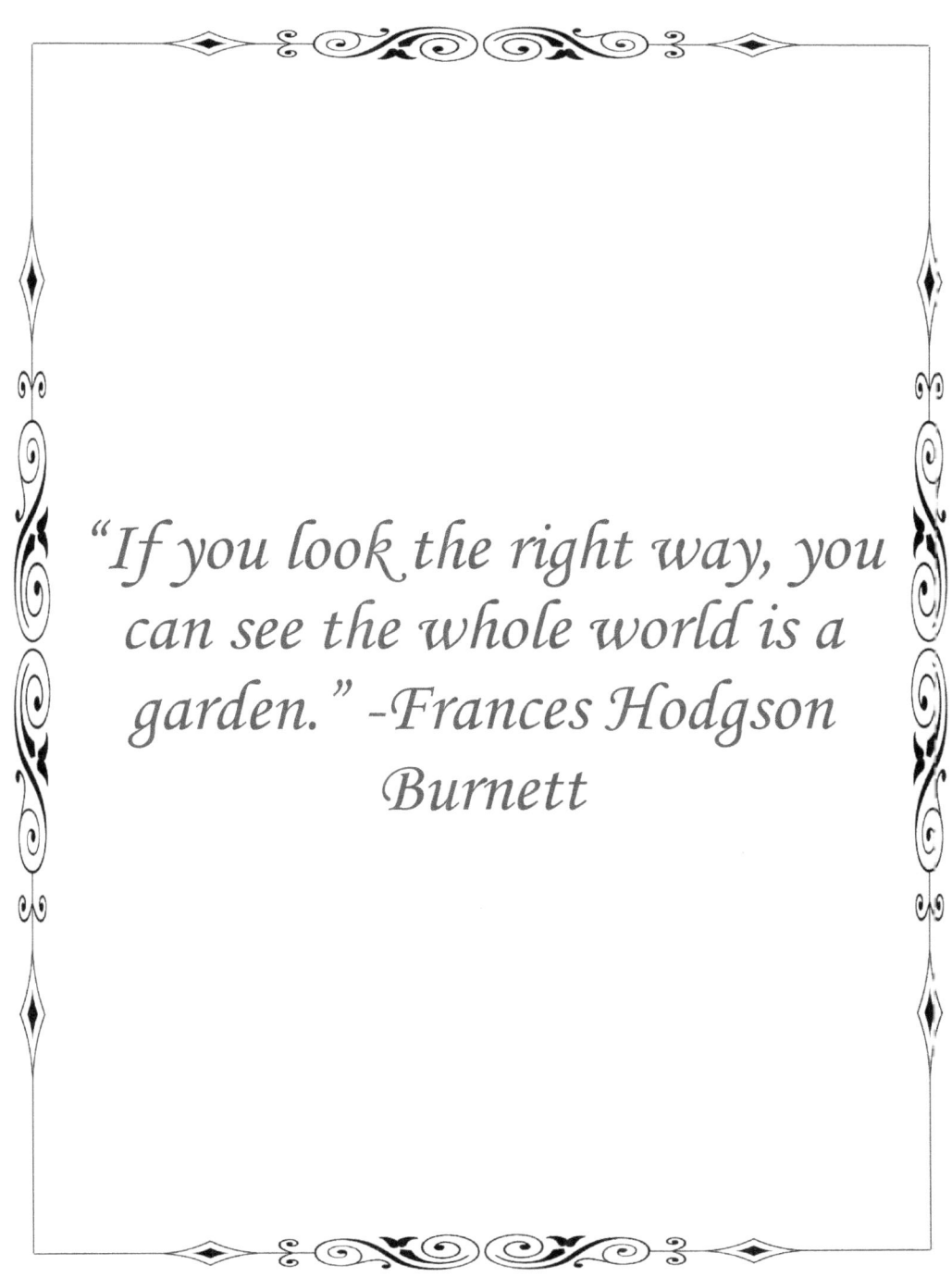

"If you look the right way, you can see the whole world is a garden." -Frances Hodgson Burnett

Your Daily Motivational Quote
Day 123

"A positive attitude causes a chain reaction of positive thoughts, events, and outcomes. It is a catalyst and it sparks extraordinary results." -Wade Boggs

Your Daily Motivational Quote
Day 124

"It's an exciting new adventure. I'm looking forward to opening a new chapter in my life." -Jane Duffield

Your Daily Motivational Quote
Day 125

"Stay positive. Stay fighting. Stay brave. Stay ambitious. Stay focused. Stay strong." -unknown

Your Daily Motivational Quote
Day 126

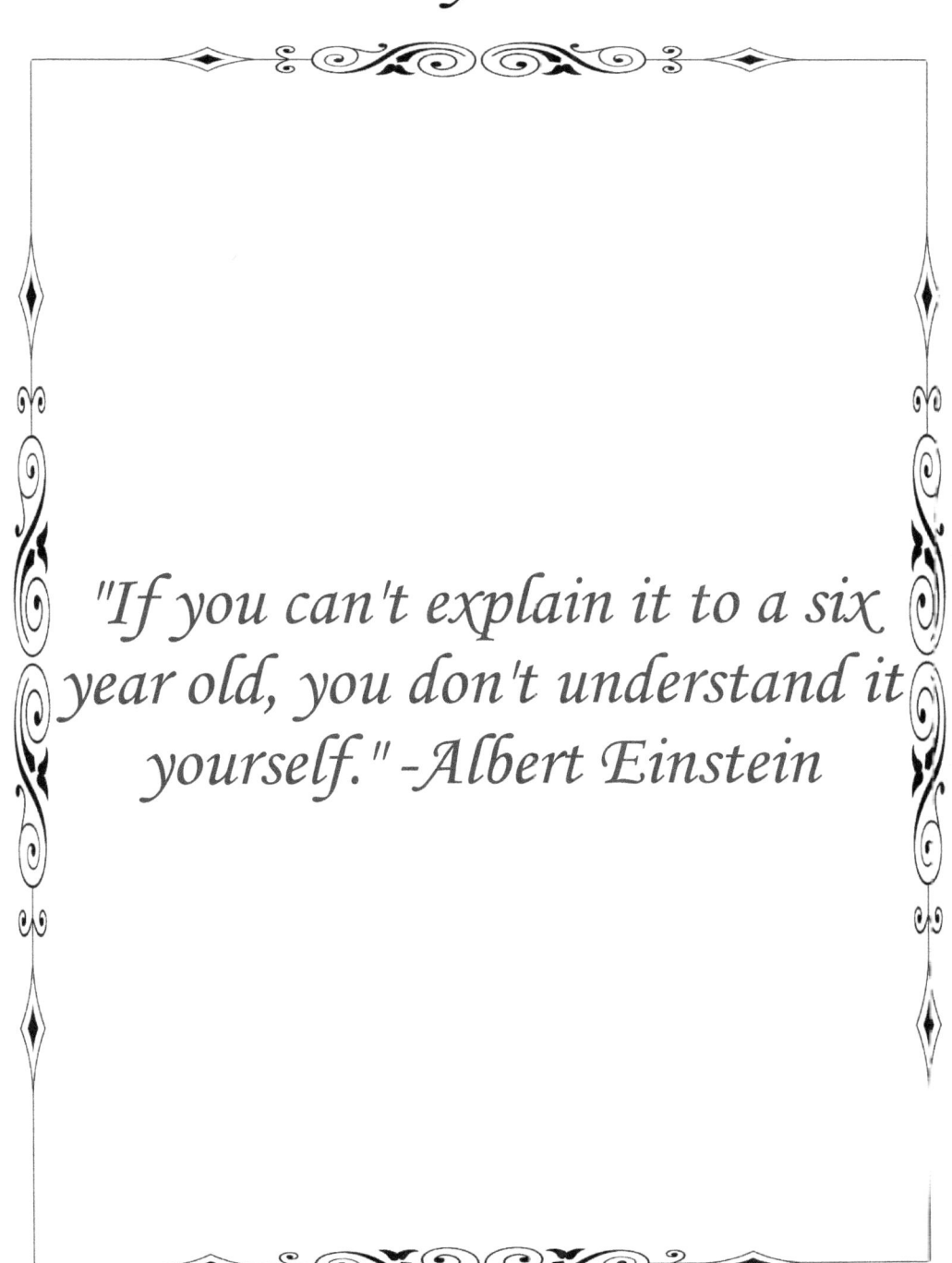

"If you can't explain it to a six year old, you don't understand it yourself." -Albert Einstein

Your Daily Motivational Quote
Day 127

"A warm smile is the universal language of kindness." -William Arthur Ward

Your Daily Motivational Quote
Day 128

"Peace is a journey of a thousand miles, and it must be taken one step at a time." -Lyndon B. Johnson

Your Daily Motivational Quote
Day 129

"Love is life. And if you miss love, you miss life." -Leo Buscaglia

Your Daily Motivational Quote
Day 130

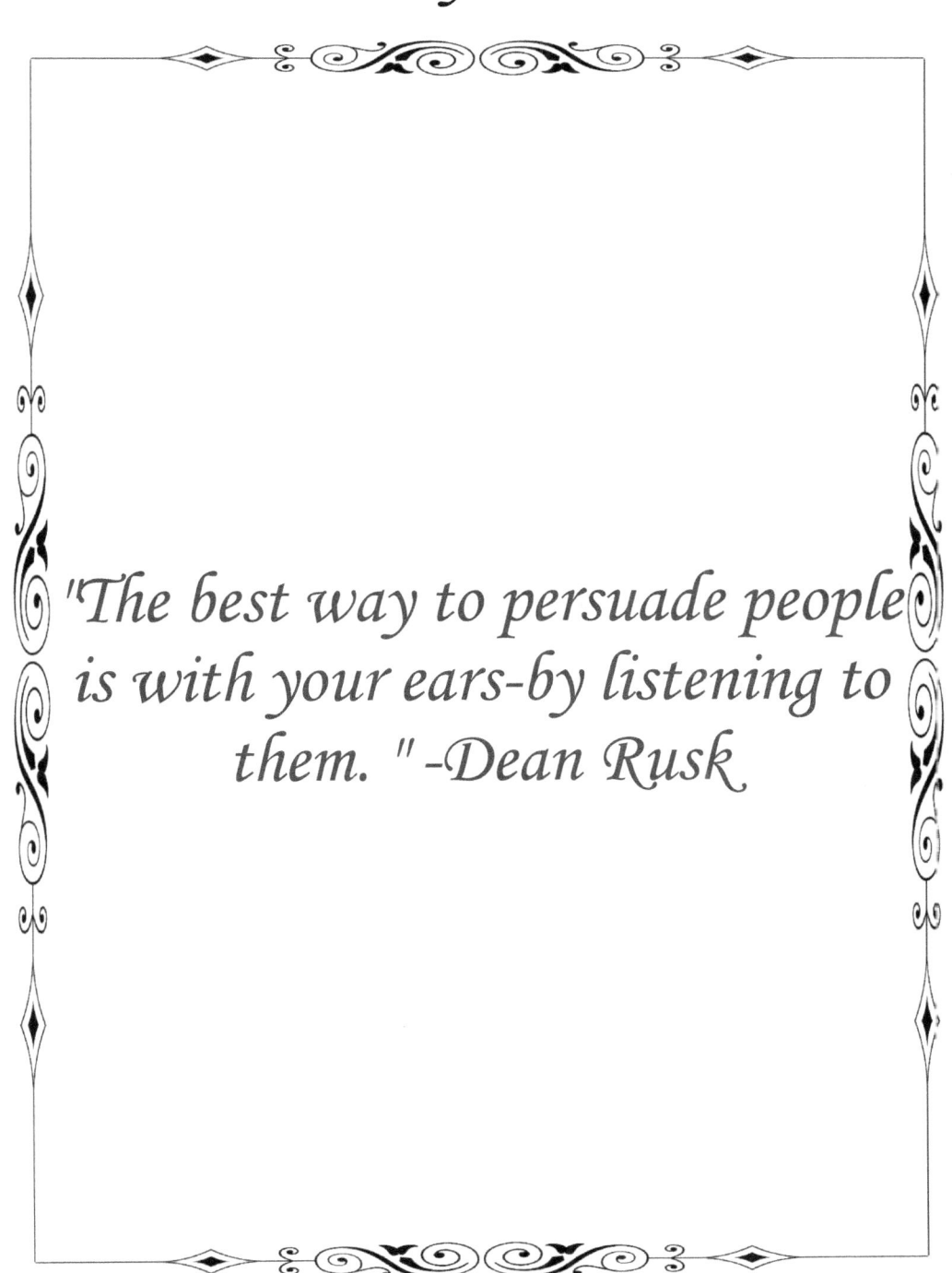

"The best way to persuade people is with your ears-by listening to them." -Dean Rusk

Your Daily Motivational Quote
Day 131

"Pride makes us artificial and humility makes us real." -Thomas Merton

Your Daily Motivational Quote
Day 132

"I've learned it's important not to limit yourself. You can do whatever you really love to do, no matter what it is." -Ryan Gosling

Your Daily Motivational Quote
Day 133

"Love begins at home, and it is not how much we do... but how much love we put in that action." -Mother Teresa

Your Daily Motivational Quote
Day 134

"Every gift from a friend is a wish for your happiness." - Richard Bach

Your Daily Motivational Quote
Day 135

"Simplicity is about subtracting the obvious and adding the meaningful." John Maeda

Your Daily Motivational Quote
Day 136

"Look up, get up, and don't ever give up." -Michael Irvin

Your Daily Motivational Quote
Day 137

"Collect things that you love, that are authentic to you, and your house becomes your story." -Erin Flett

Your Daily Motivational Quote
Day 138

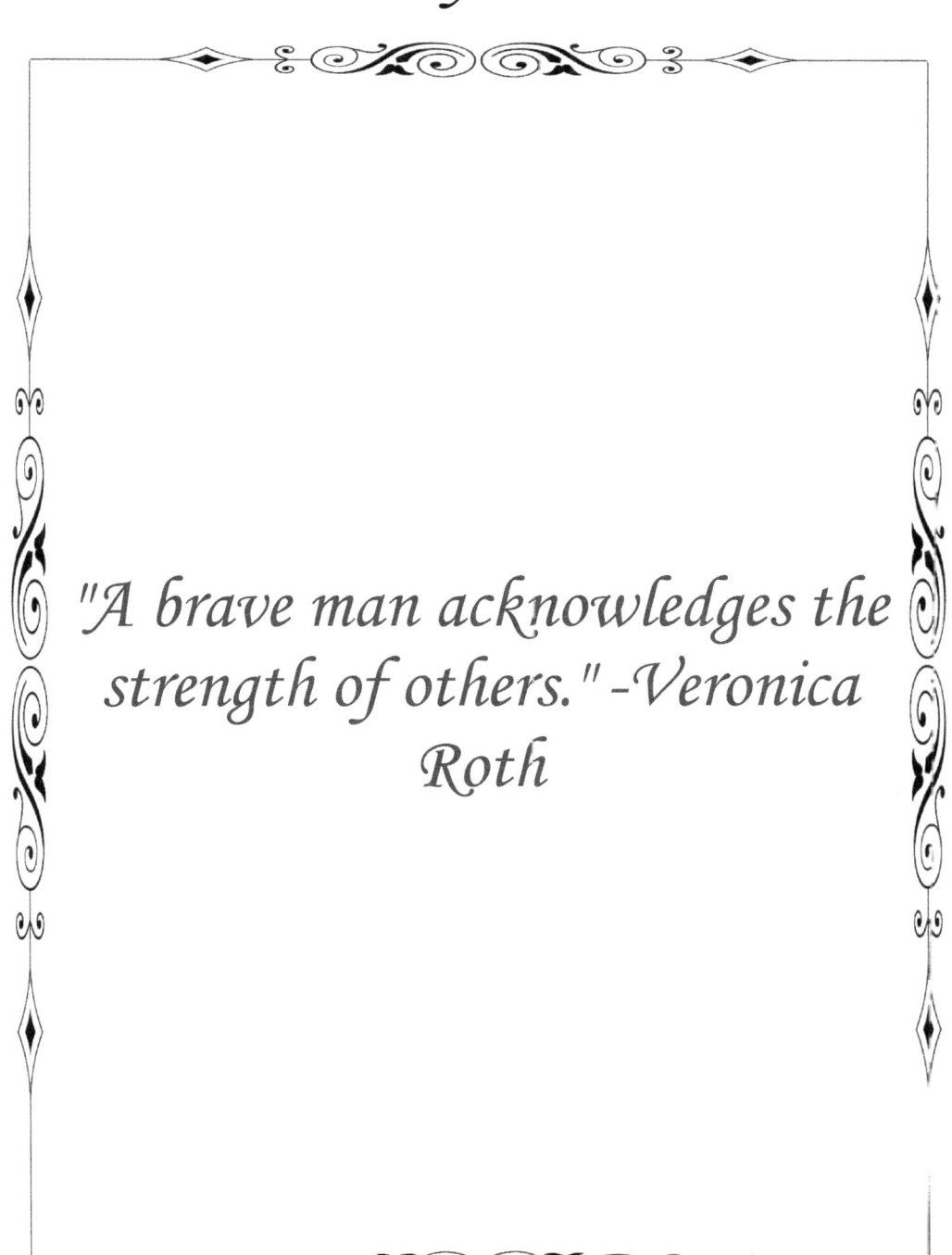

"A brave man acknowledges the strength of others." -Veronica Roth

Your Daily Motivational Quote
Day 139

"You have to dream before your dreams can come true." -A.P.J. Abdul Kalam

Your Daily Motivational Quote
Day 140

"Be strong. Live honorably and with dignity. When you don't think you can, hold on." -James Frey

Your Daily Motivational Quote
Day 141

"Give every day the chance to be the most beautiful day in your life." -Mark Twain

Your Daily Motivational Quote
Day 142

"Most people do not listen with the intent to understand; they listen with the intent to reply." - Stephen R. Covey

Your Daily Motivational Quote
Day 143

"Forgiveness is a gift you give yourself." -Suzanne Somers

Your Daily Motivational Quote
Day 144

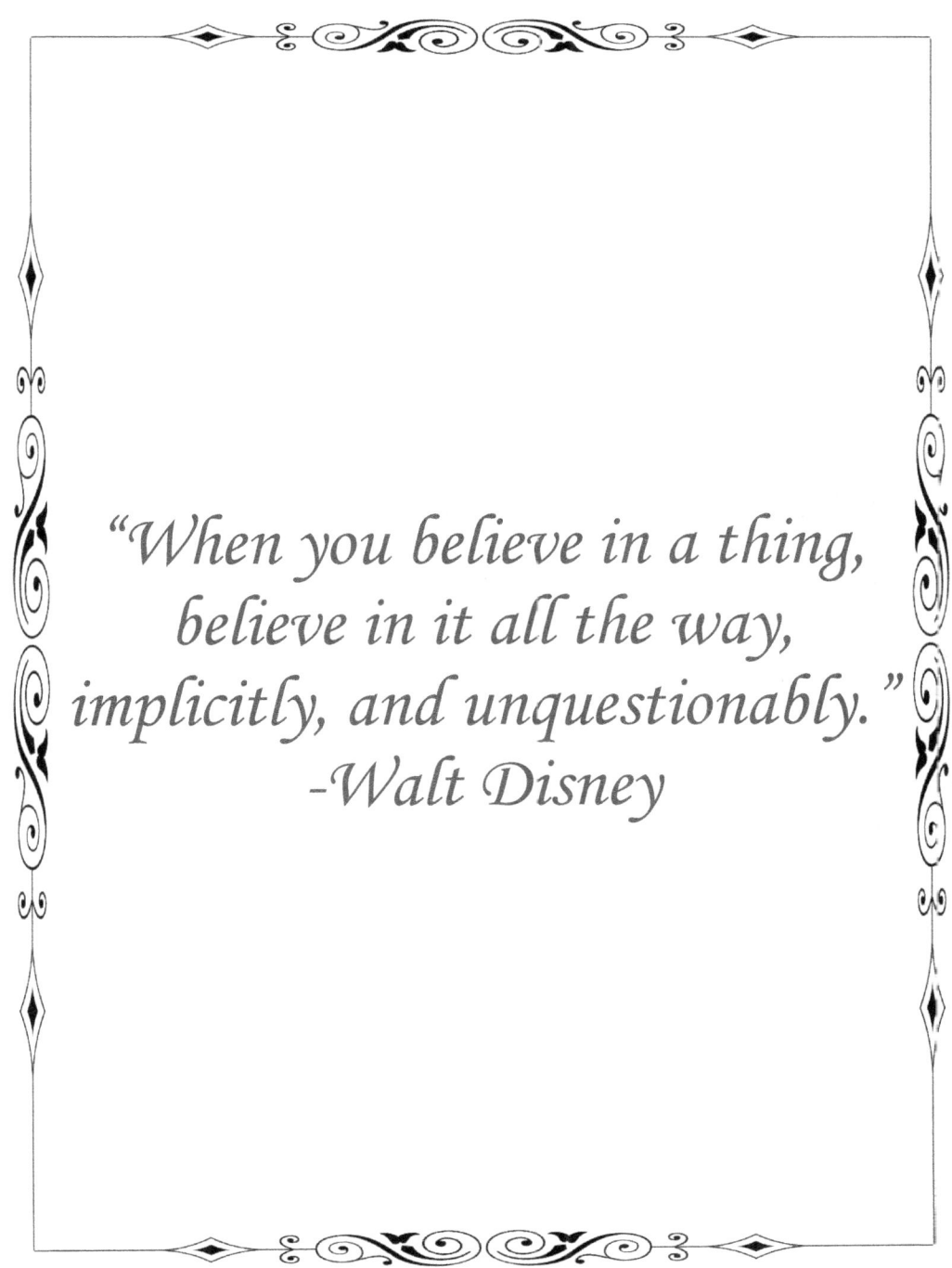

"When you believe in a thing, believe in it all the way, implicitly, and unquestionably."
-Walt Disney

Your Daily Motivational Quote
Day 145

"If you feel like there's something out there that you're supposed to be doing, if you have a passion for it, then stop wishing and just do it." -Wanda Skyes

Your Daily Motivational Quote
Day 146

"Life is really simple, but we insist on making it complicated." - Aristotle

Your Daily Motivational Quote
Day 147

"Love yourself and love your body because it's perfect the way it is. You don't have to be someone else's version of beautiful to be truly beautiful." - Jessica Steele

Your Daily Motivational Quote
Day 148

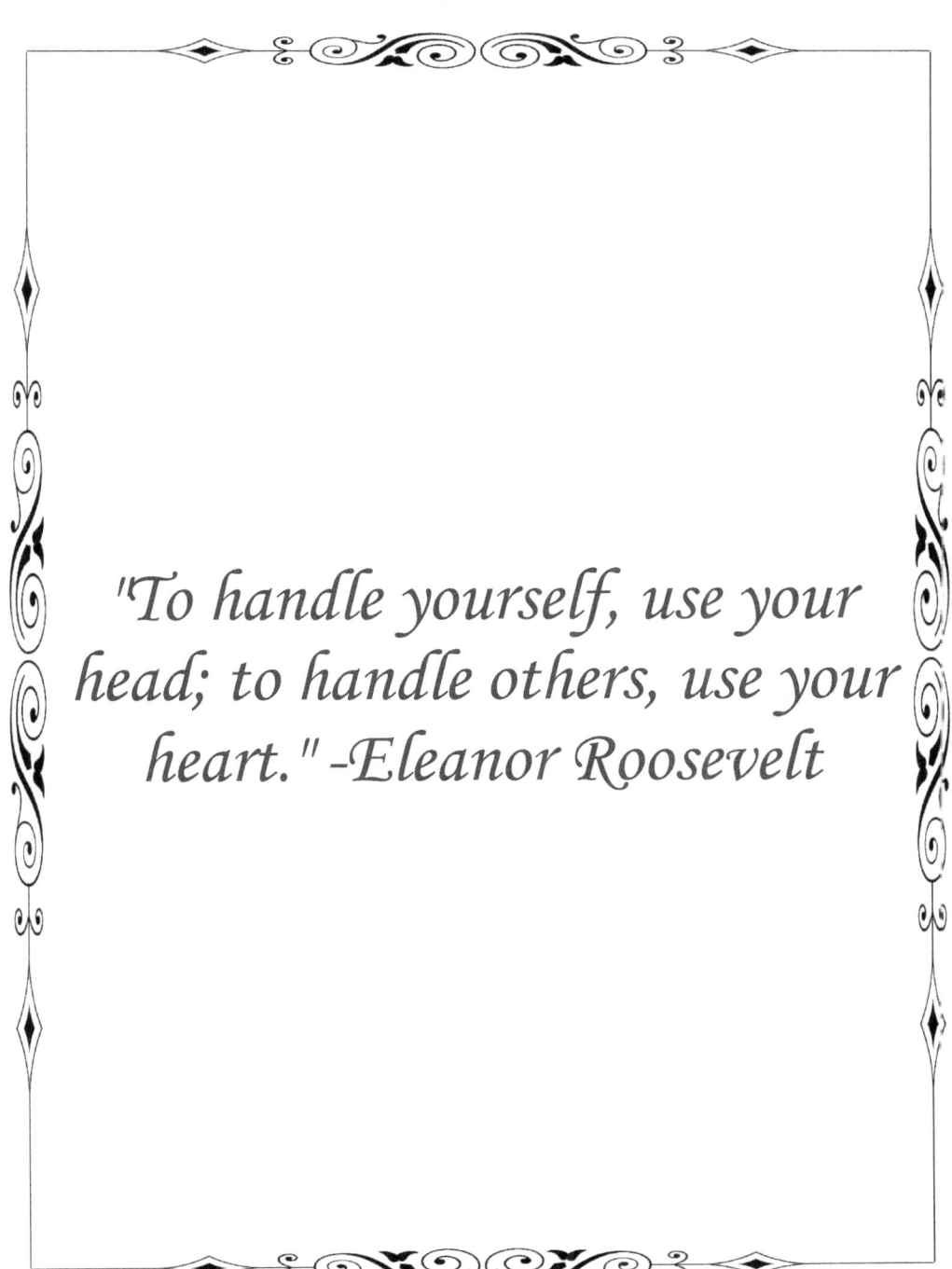

"To handle yourself, use your head; to handle others, use your heart." -Eleanor Roosevelt

Your Daily Motivational Quote
Day 149

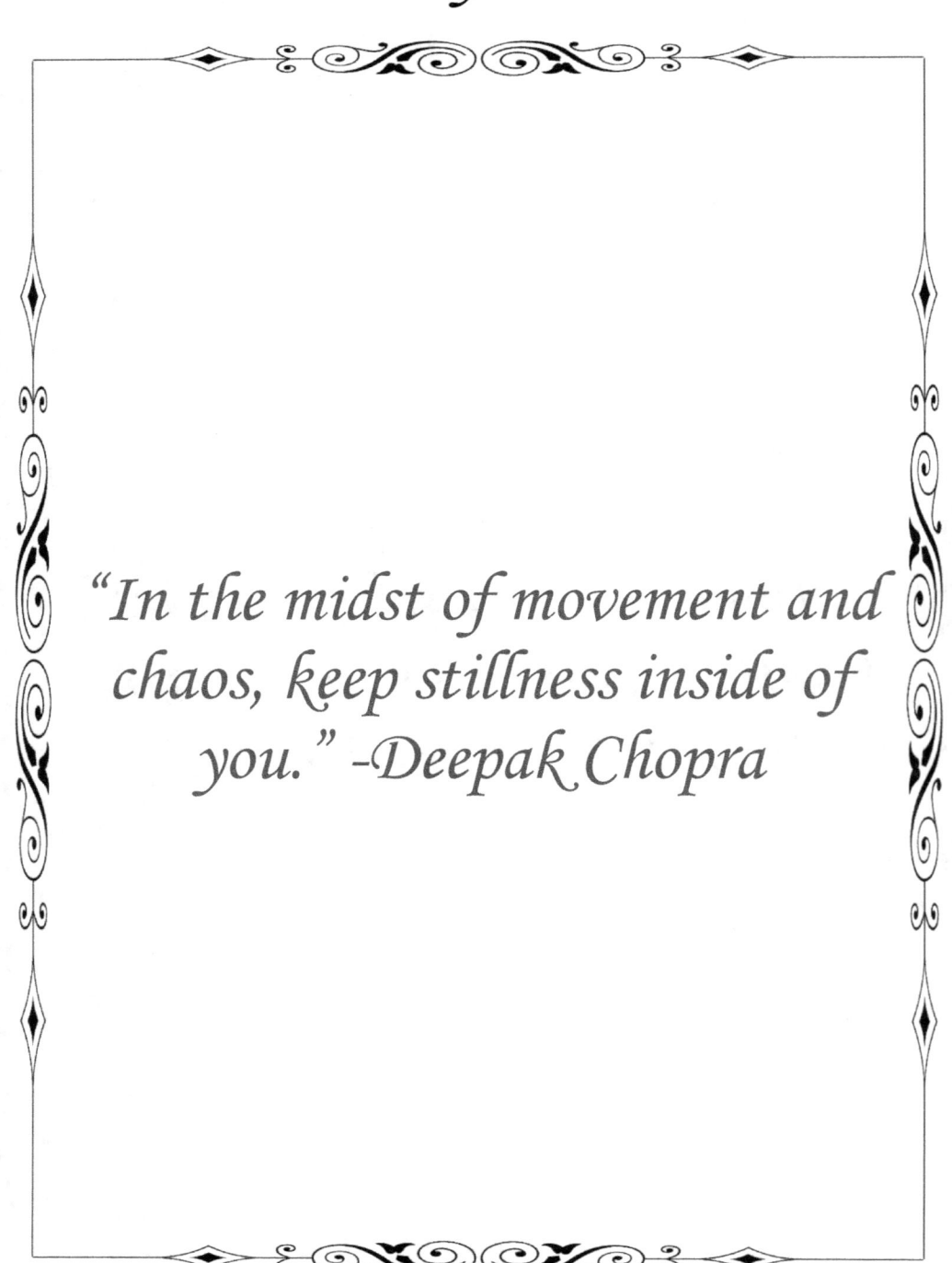

"In the midst of movement and chaos, keep stillness inside of you." -Deepak Chopra

Your Daily Motivational Quote
Day 150

"Running is about finding your inner peace, and so is a life well lived… Run with your heart." - Dean Karnazes

Your Daily Motivational Quote
Day 151

"Nothing is as important as passion. No matter what you want to do with your life, be passionate." -Jon Bon Jovi

Your Daily Motivational Quote
Day 152

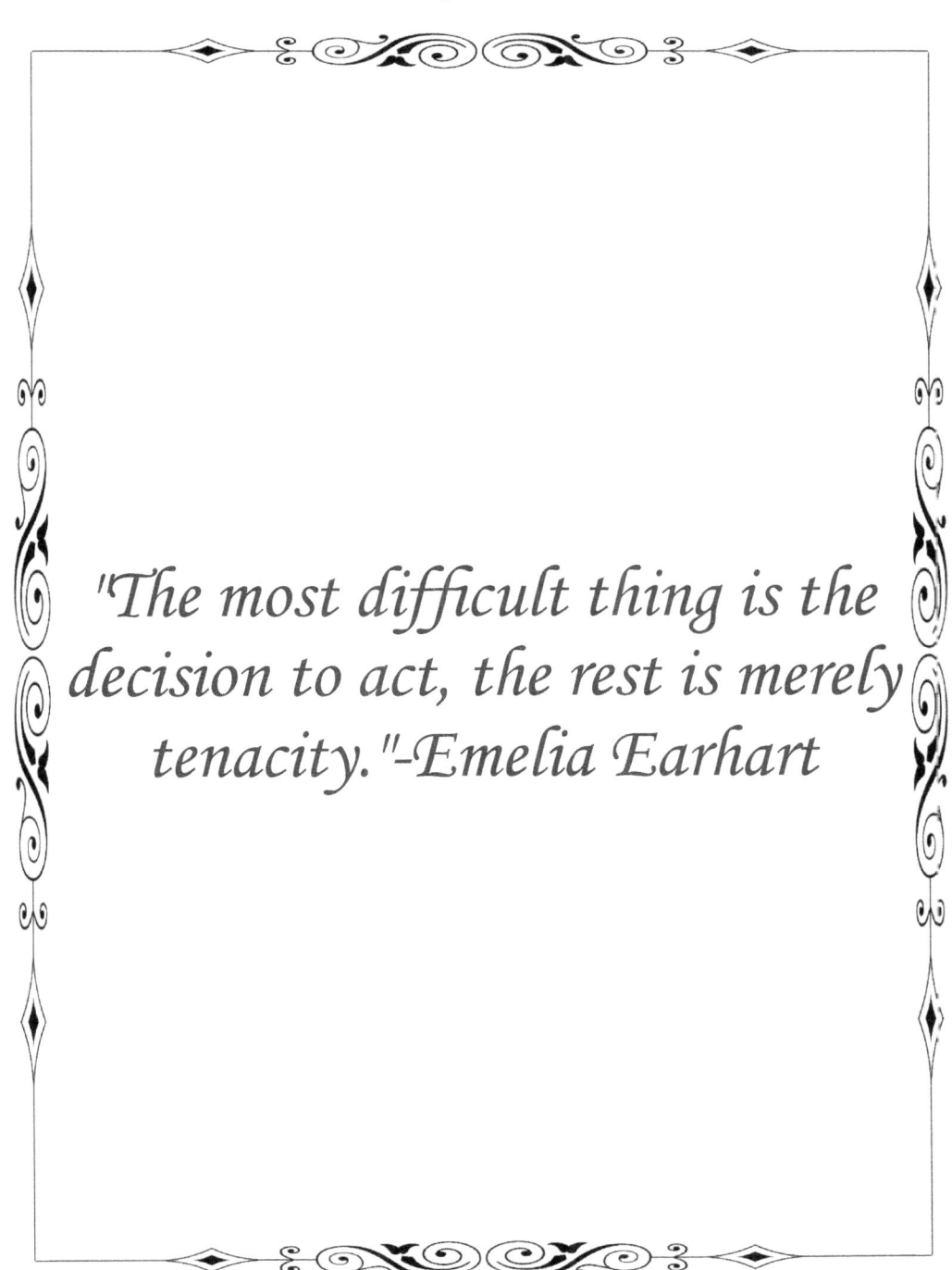

"The most difficult thing is the decision to act, the rest is merely tenacity." -Emelia Earhart

Your Daily Motivational Quote
Day 153

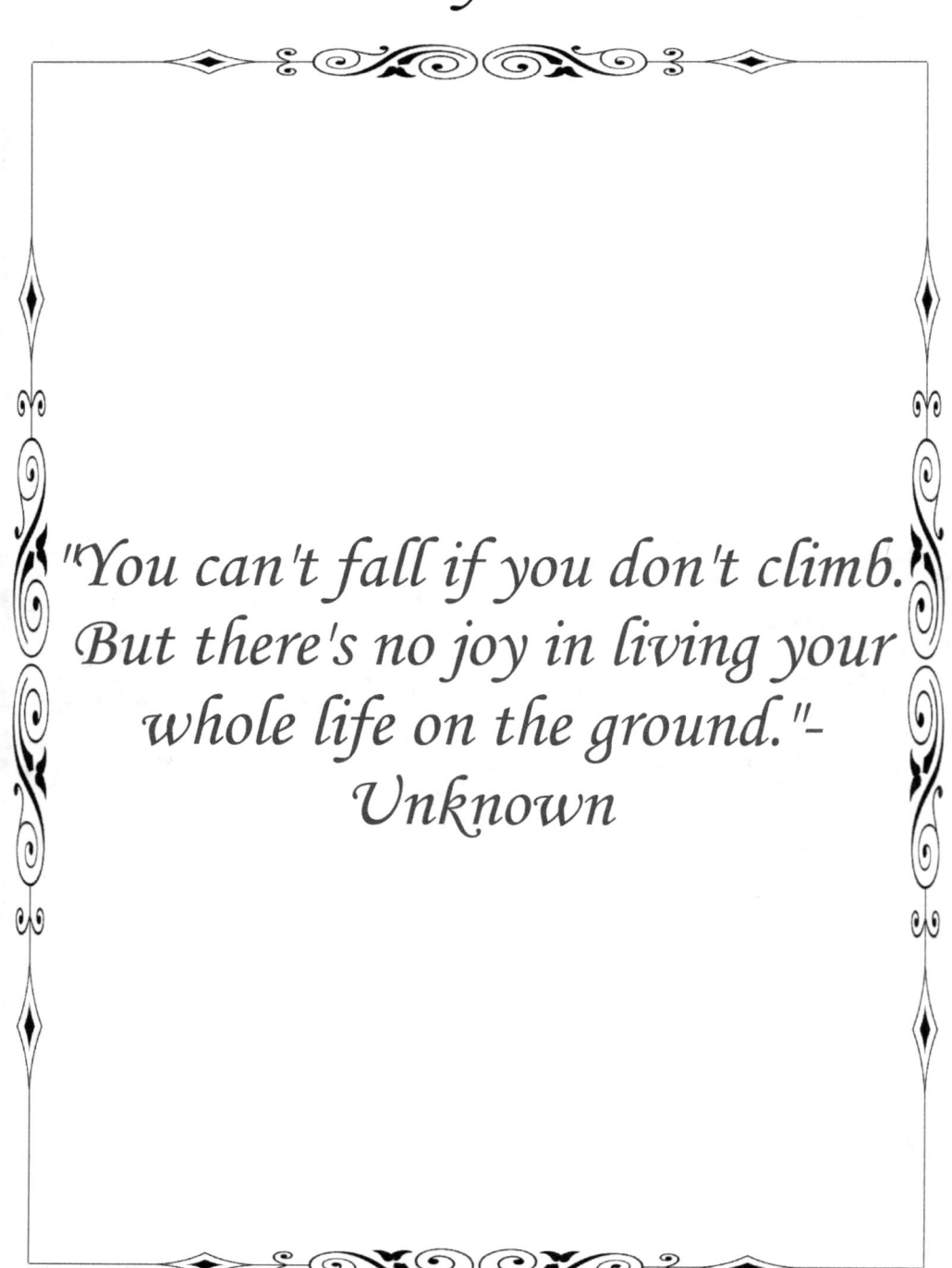

"You can't fall if you don't climb. But there's no joy in living your whole life on the ground."- Unknown

Your Daily Motivational Quote
Day 154

"Be always blooming." - unknown

Your Daily Motivational Quote
Day 155

"Think of all the beauty still left around you and be happy." - Anne Frank

Your Daily Motivational Quote
Day 156

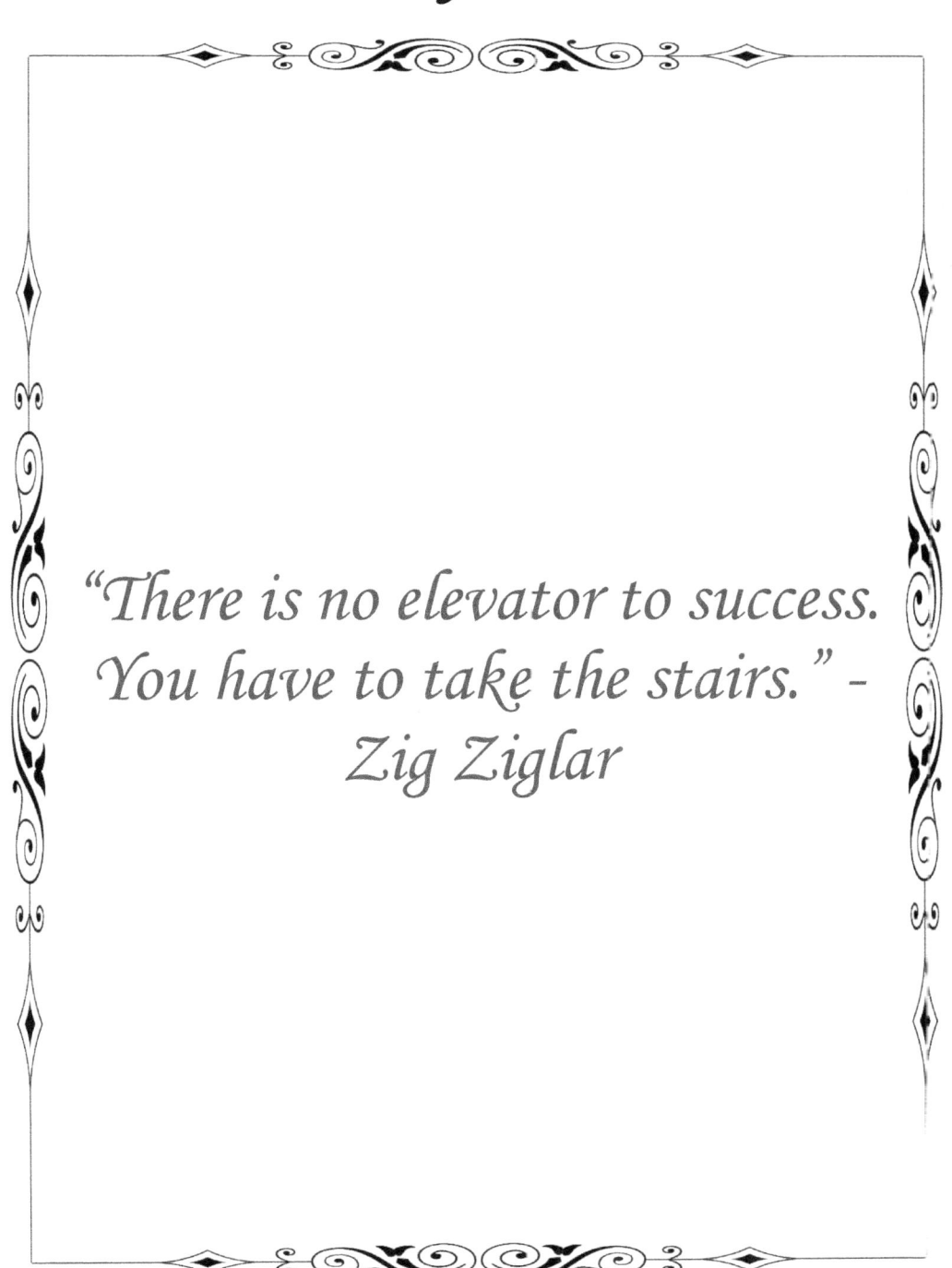

"There is no elevator to success. You have to take the stairs." - Zig Ziglar

Your Daily Motivational Quote
Day 157

"A flower cannot blossom without sunshine, and man cannot live without love." -Max Muller

Your Daily Motivational Quote
Day 158

"Kindness is a language which the deaf can hear and the blind can see." -Mark Twain

Your Daily Motivational Quote
Day 159

"Sometimes a change of perspective is all it takes to see the light." -Dan Brown

Your Daily Motivational Quote
Day 160

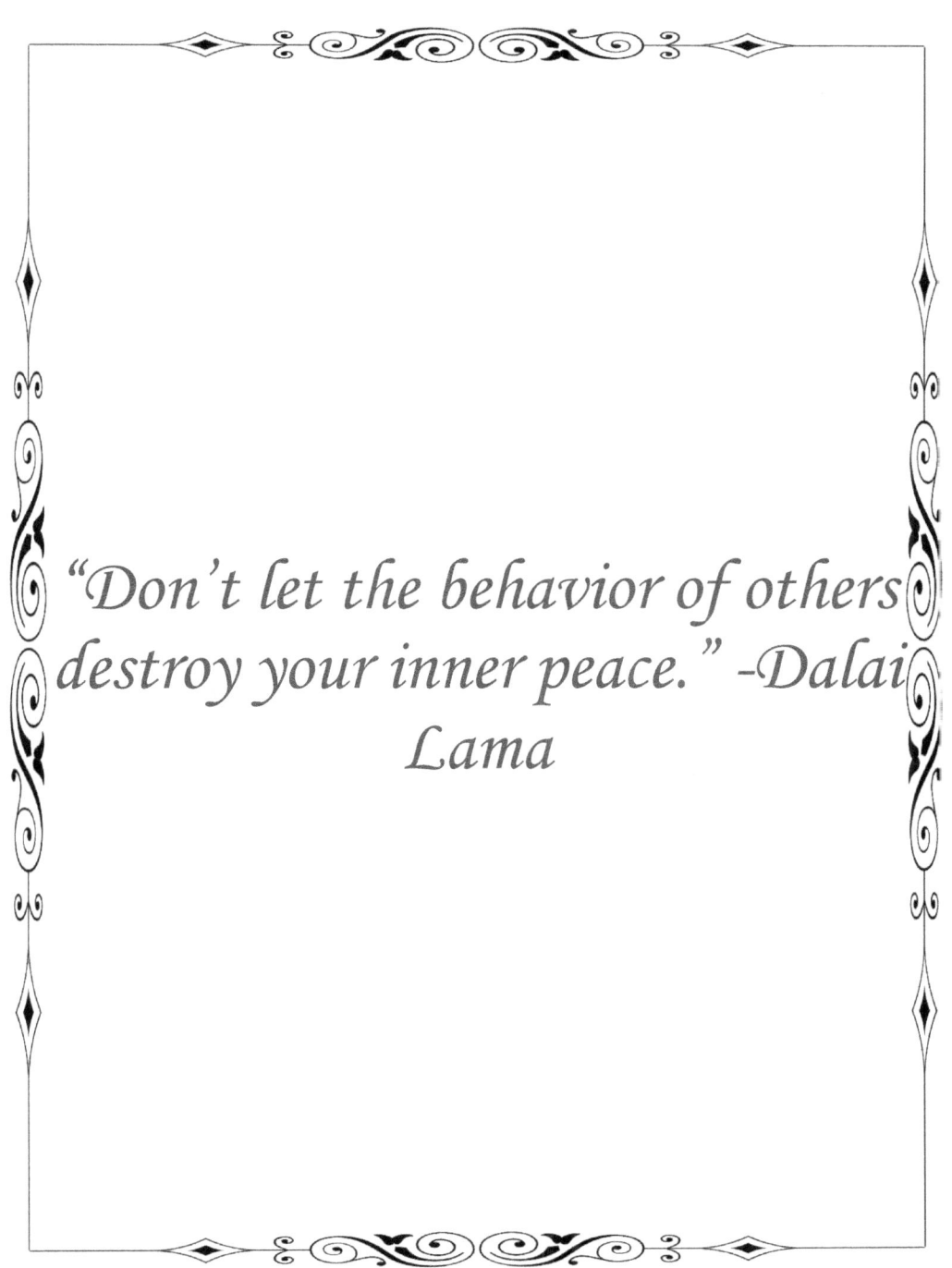

"Don't let the behavior of others destroy your inner peace." -Dalai Lama

Your Daily Motivational Quote
Day 161

"Education is the most powerful weapon which you can use to change the world." -Nelson Mandela

Your Daily Motivational Quote
Day 162

"Being different simply means you have something unique to offer the world." -Scarlett Vespa

Your Daily Motivational Quote
Day 163

"Wherever you go, go with all your heart." -Confucius

Your Daily Motivational Quote
Day 164

"Symmetry is what we see at a glance." -Blaise Pascal

Your Daily Motivational Quote
Day 165

"Beauty is about enhancing what you have. Let yourself shine through." -Janelle Monae

Your Daily Motivational Quote
Day 166

"I have made mistakes, but I have never made the mistake of claiming that I never made one."
-James Gordon Bennett

Your Daily Motivational Quote
Day 167

"Faith makes all things possible... love makes all things easy." -Dwight L. Moody

Your Daily Motivational Quote
Day 168

"Tactics, fitness, stroke ability, adaptability, experience, and sportsmanship are all necessary for winning." -Fred Perry

Your Daily Motivational Quote
Day 169

"Success is almost totally dependent upon drive and persistence. The extra energy required to make another effort or try another approach is the secret of winning." -Denis Waitley

Your Daily Motivational Quote
Day 170

"When I meet successful people I ask 100 questions as to what they attribute their success to. It is usually the same: persistence, hard work and hiring good people." -Kiana Tom

Your Daily Motivational Quote
Day 171

"Surprise yourself every day with your own courage." -Denholm Elliott

Your Daily Motivational Quote
Day 172

"Don't wait for other people to be loving, giving, compassionate, grateful, forgiving, generous, or friendly... lead the way!" -Steve Maraboli

Your Daily Motivational Quote
Day 173

"Adaptability is about the powerful difference between adapting to cope and adapting to win." -Max McKeown

Your Daily Motivational Quote
Day 174

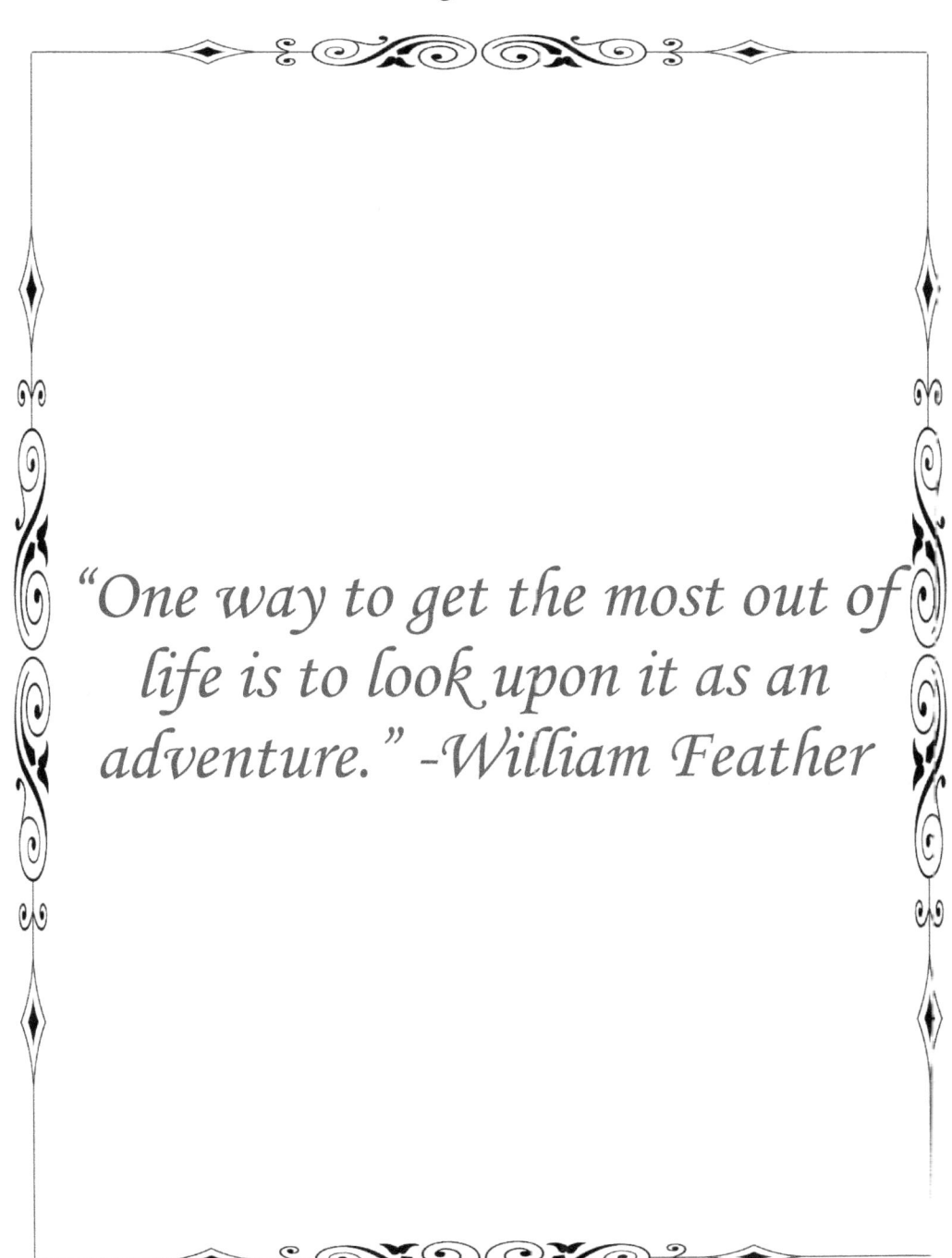

"One way to get the most out of life is to look upon it as an adventure." -William Feather

Your Daily Motivational Quote
Day 175

"To live is the rarest thing in the world. Most people exist, that is all." Oscar Wilde

Your Daily Motivational Quote
Day 176

"When people talk, listen completely. Most people never listen." -Ernest Hemingway

Your Daily Motivational Quote
Day 177

"Alone we can do so little, together we can do so much." - Helen Keller

Your Daily Motivational Quote
Day 178

"Blue skies smiling at me.
Nothing but blue skies do I see."
-Irving Berlin

Your Daily Motivational Quote
Day 179

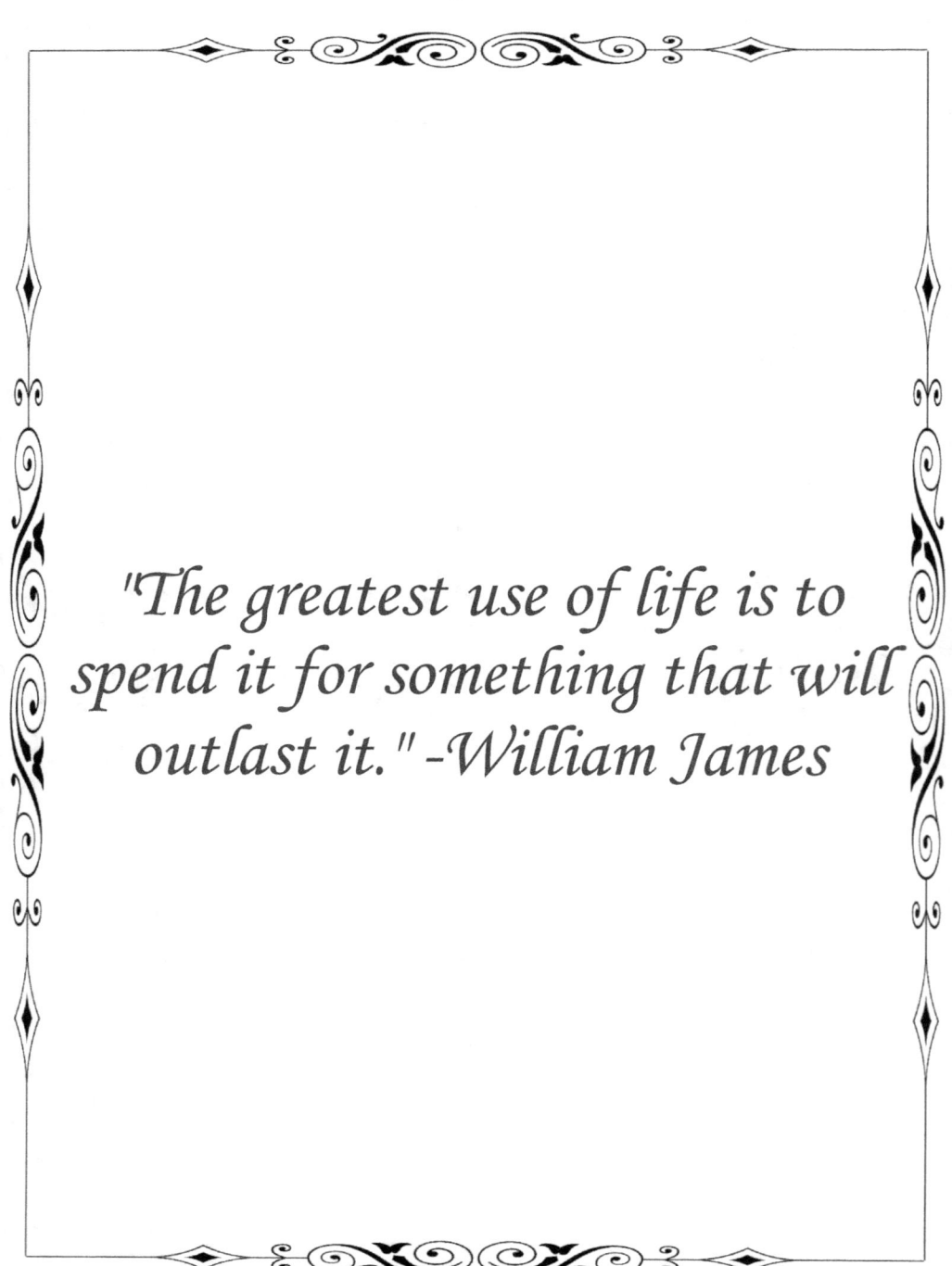

"The greatest use of life is to spend it for something that will outlast it." -William James

Your Daily Motivational Quote
Day 180

"Almost everything will work again if you unplug it for a few minutes… including you." - Anne Lamott

Your Daily Motivational Quote
Day 181

"It's weird that the greatest moments of clarity occur during moments of such confusion and stress." -Nishan Panwar

Your Daily Motivational Quote
Day 182

"Not everything that is faced can be changed, but nothing can be changed until it is faced." - James Baldwin

Your Daily Motivational Quote
Day 183

"The future belongs to those who believe in the beauty of their dreams." -Eleanor Roosevelt

Your Daily Motivational Quote
Day 184

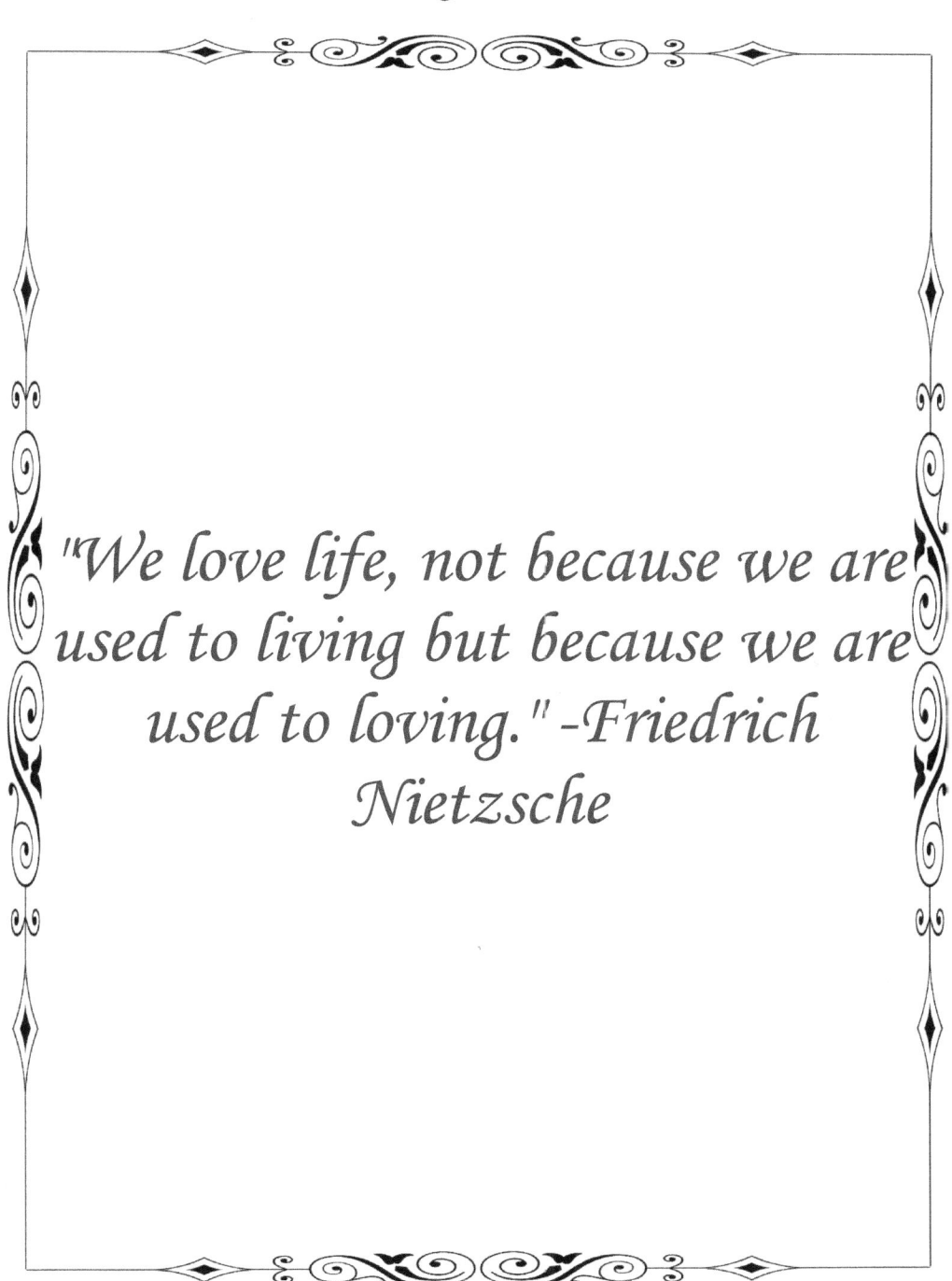

"We love life, not because we are used to living but because we are used to loving." -Friedrich Nietzsche

Your Daily Motivational Quote
Day 185

"Change your thoughts and you change your world." -Norman Vincent Peale

Your Daily Motivational Quote
Day 186

"With the new day comes new strength and new thoughts." - Eleanor Roosevelt

Your Daily Motivational Quote
Day 187

"Life in abundance comes only through great love." -Elbert Hubbard

Your Daily Motivational Quote
Day 188

"Wisdom is the reward you get for a lifetime of listening when you'd have preferred to talk." - Doug Larson

Your Daily Motivational Quote
Day 189

"May you be happy always." - Honore de Balzac

Your Daily Motivational Quote
Day 190

"Once in a while, right in the middle of an ordinary life, love gives us a fairy tale." -unknown

Your Daily Motivational Quote
Day 191

"Wherever there is a human being, there is an opportunity for a kindness." -Lucius Annaeus Seneca

Your Daily Motivational Quote
Day 192

"Treat everyone with respect and kindness. Period. No exceptions."
-Kiana Tom

Your Daily Motivational Quote
Day 193

"Listening is being able to be changed by the other person." - Alan Alda

Your Daily Motivational Quote
Day 194

"Sometimes reality is too complex. Stories give it form." - Jean Luc Godard

Your Daily Motivational Quote
Day 195

"Always be a first-rate version of yourself and not a second-rate version of someone else." -Judy Garland

Your Daily Motivational Quote
Day 196

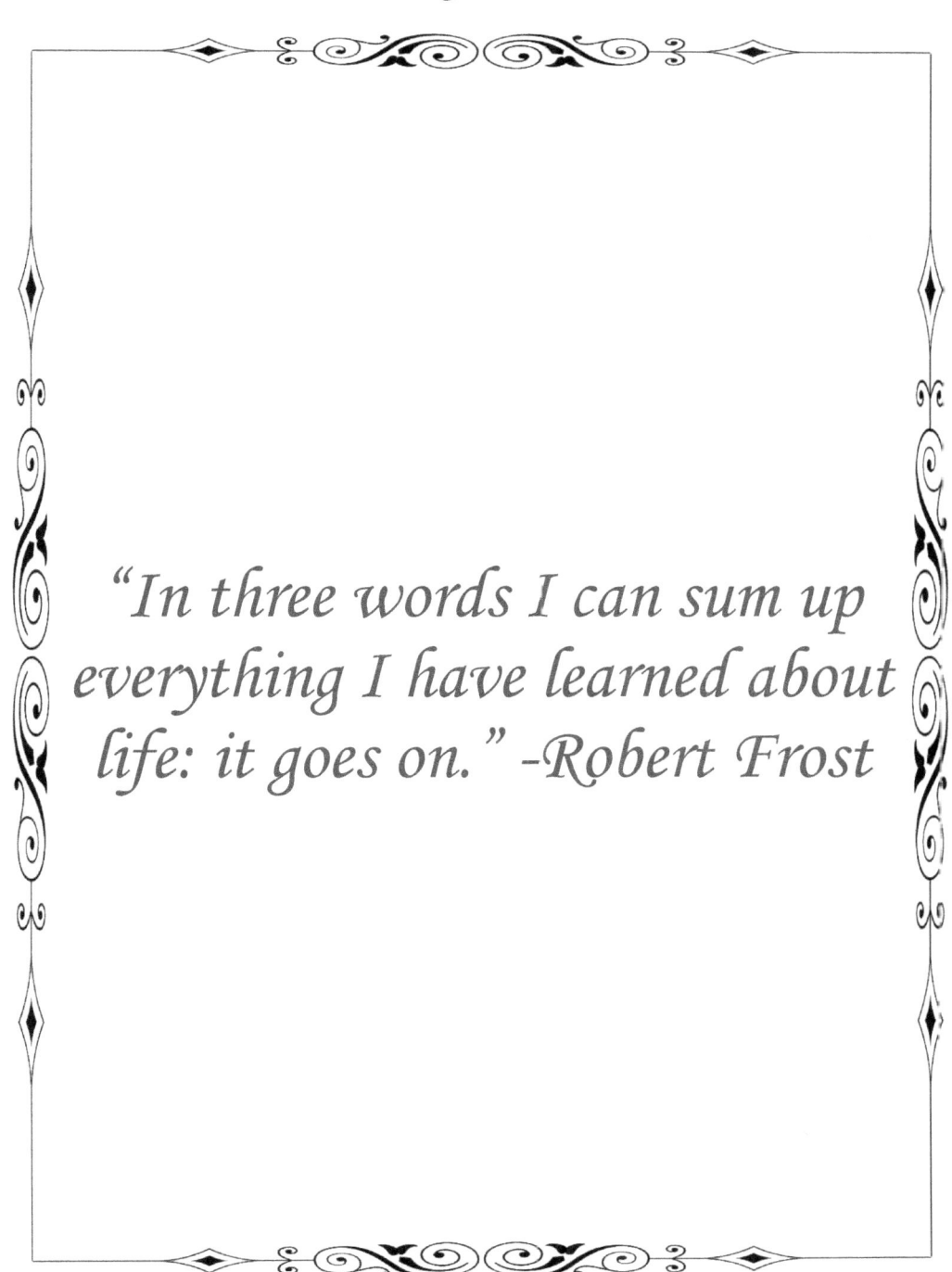

"In three words I can sum up everything I have learned about life: it goes on." -Robert Frost

Your Daily Motivational Quote
Day 197

"Transparency, honesty, kindness, good stewardship, even humor, work in businesses at all times." -John Gerzema

Your Daily Motivational Quote
Day 198

"Remember teamwork begins by building trust. And the only way to do that is to overcome our need for invulnerability." - Patrick Lencioni

Your Daily Motivational Quote
Day 199

"Relax & clear your mind if someone is speaking, so that you're receptive to what they're saying."-Roger Ailes

Your Daily Motivational Quote
Day 200

"Every great dream begins with a dreamer. Always remember, you have within you the strength, the patience, and the passion to reach for the stars to change the world." -Harriet Tubman

Your Daily Motivational Quote
Day 201

"Things change. And friends leave. Life doesn't stop for anybody." -Stephen Chbosky

Your Daily Motivational Quote
Day 202

"I work very hard, and I play very hard. I'm grateful for life. And I live it-I believe life loves the liver of it. I live it." -Maya Angelou

Your Daily Motivational Quote
Day 203

"The earth has its music for those who will listen." -George Santayana

Your Daily Motivational Quote
Day 204

"Life isn't about waiting for the storm to pass. It's about learning how to dance in the rain." - Vivian Greene

Your Daily Motivational Quote
Day 205

"Do not go where the path may lead, instead go where there is no path and leave a trail." -Ralph Waldo Emerson

Your Daily Motivational Quote
Day 206

"Nobody can make you happy until you're happy with yourself first." -unknown

Your Daily Motivational Quote
Day 207

"*I have plenty to look forward to, I'm sure.*" -Miranda Otto

Your Daily Motivational Quote
Day 208

"Your spark can become a flame and change everything." -E.D. Nixon

Your Daily Motivational Quote
Day 209

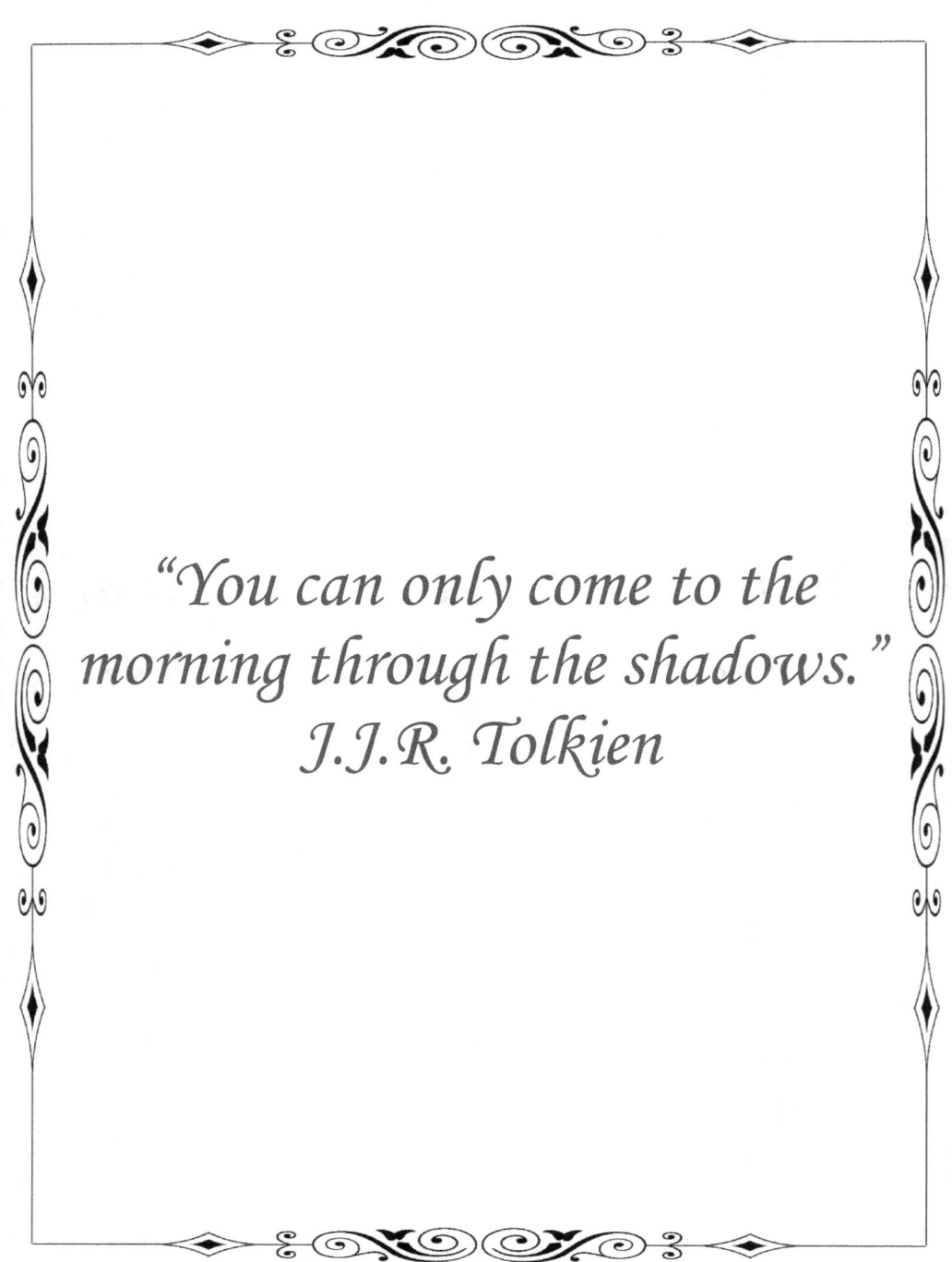

"You can only come to the morning through the shadows."
J.J.R. Tolkien

Your Daily Motivational Quote
Day 210

"Kindness is like snow—it beautifies everything it covers." - Kahlil Gibran

Your Daily Motivational Quote
Day 211

"The most important thing in communication is hearing what isn't said" -Peter Drucker

Your Daily Motivational Quote
Day 212

"Home is where your heart is." - unknown

Your Daily Motivational Quote
Day 213

"The best proof of love is trust." - Joyce Brothers

Your Daily Motivational Quote
Day 214

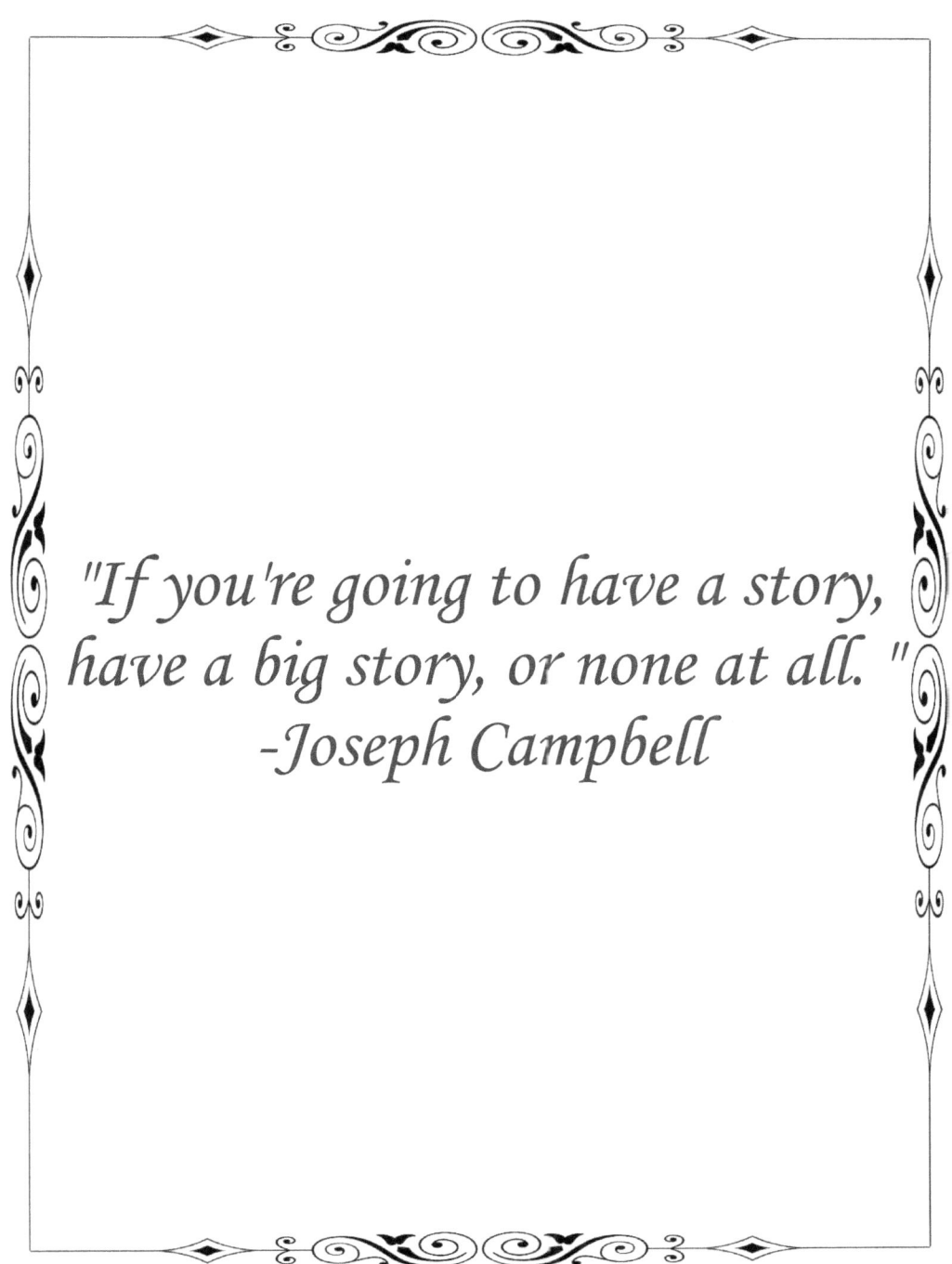

"If you're going to have a story, have a big story, or none at all."
-Joseph Campbell

Your Daily Motivational Quote
Day 215

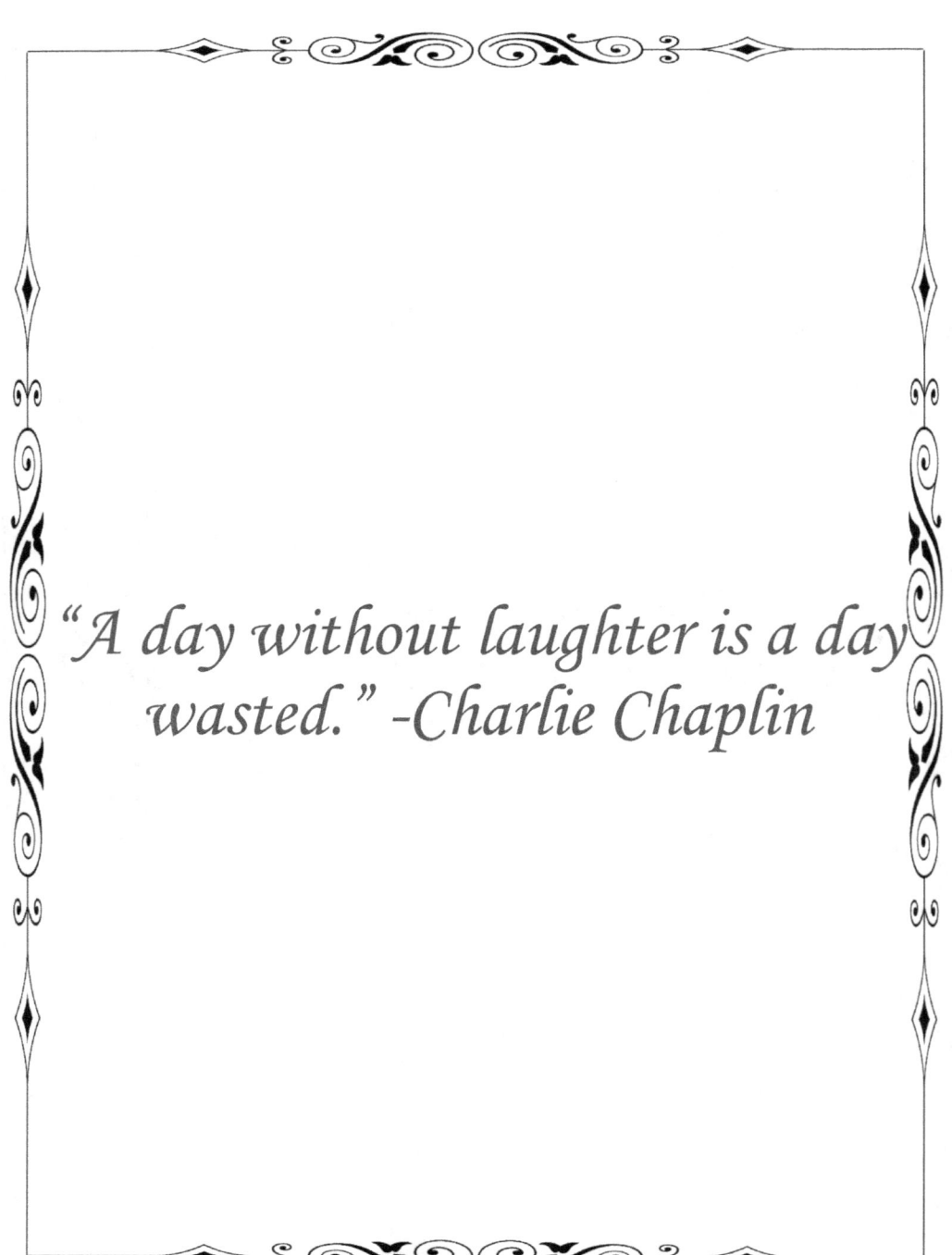

"A day without laughter is a day wasted." -Charlie Chaplin

Your Daily Motivational Quote
Day 216

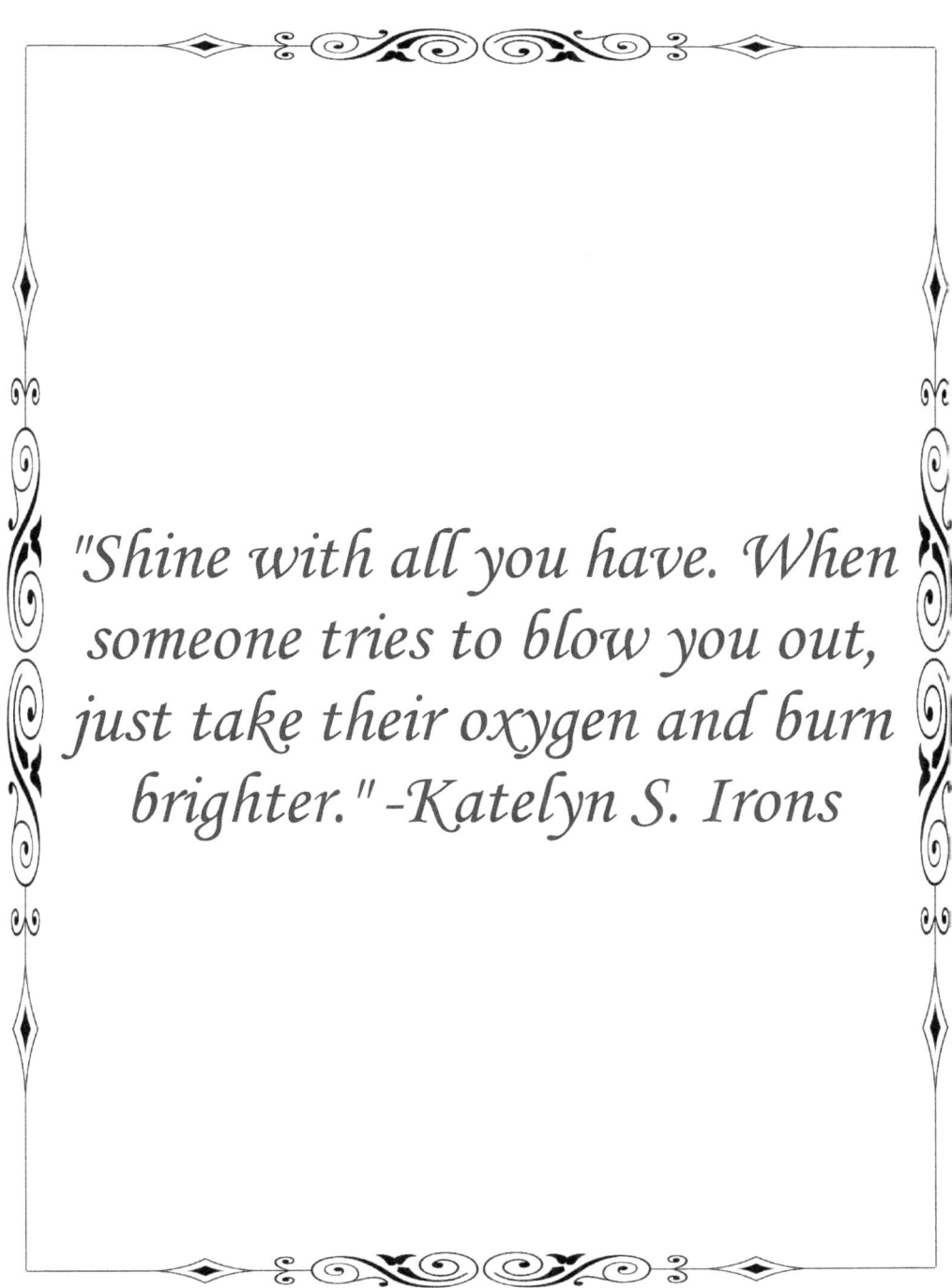

"Shine with all you have. When someone tries to blow you out, just take their oxygen and burn brighter." -Katelyn S. Irons

Your Daily Motivational Quote
Day 217

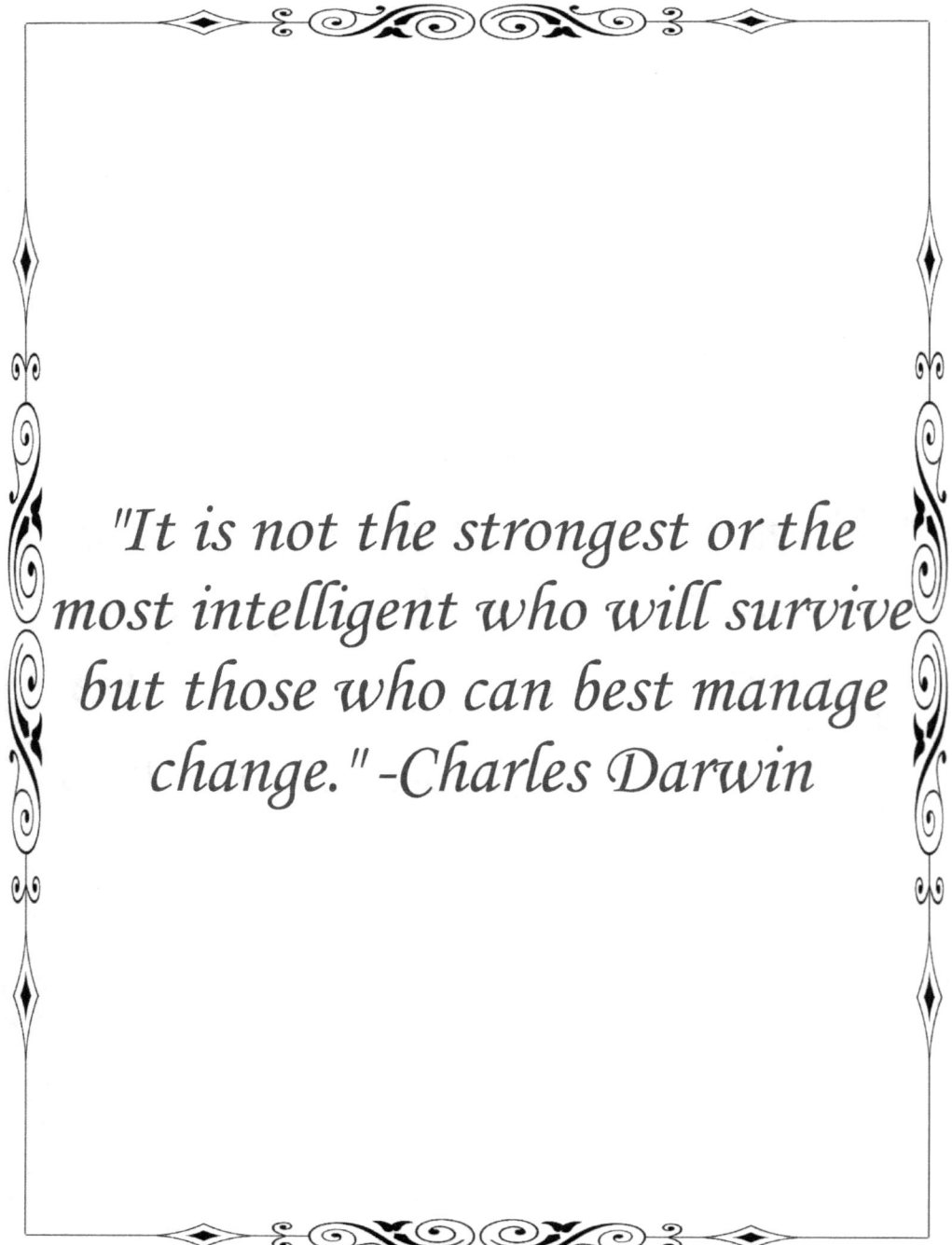

"It is not the strongest or the most intelligent who will survive but those who can best manage change." -Charles Darwin

Your Daily Motivational Quote
Day 218

"Explore. Dream. Discover." - Mark Twain

Your Daily Motivational Quote
Day 219

"It doesn't take much to surprise others, but to surprise oneself- now that is a great feat." - Kristen Hartley

Your Daily Motivational Quote
Day 220

"Simplicity and repose are the qualities that measure the true value of any work of art." - Frank Lloyd Wright

Your Daily Motivational Quote
Day 221

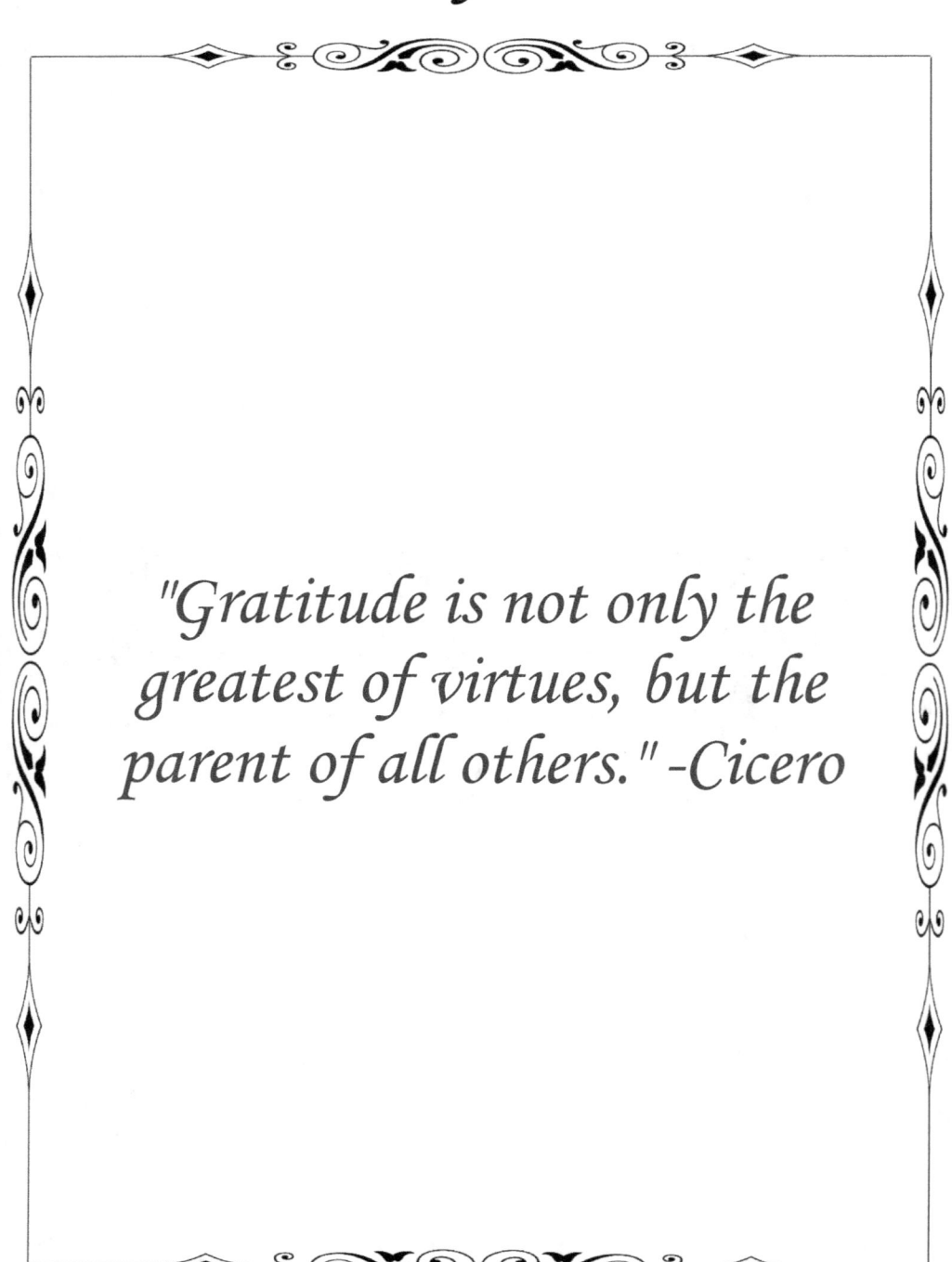

"Gratitude is not only the greatest of virtues, but the parent of all others." -Cicero

Your Daily Motivational Quote
Day 222

"When the need to succeed is as bad as the need to breathe, then you'll be successful." -Eric Thomas

Your Daily Motivational Quote
Day 223

"Never lose a chance of saying a kind word." -William Makepeace Thackeray

Your Daily Motivational Quote
Day 224

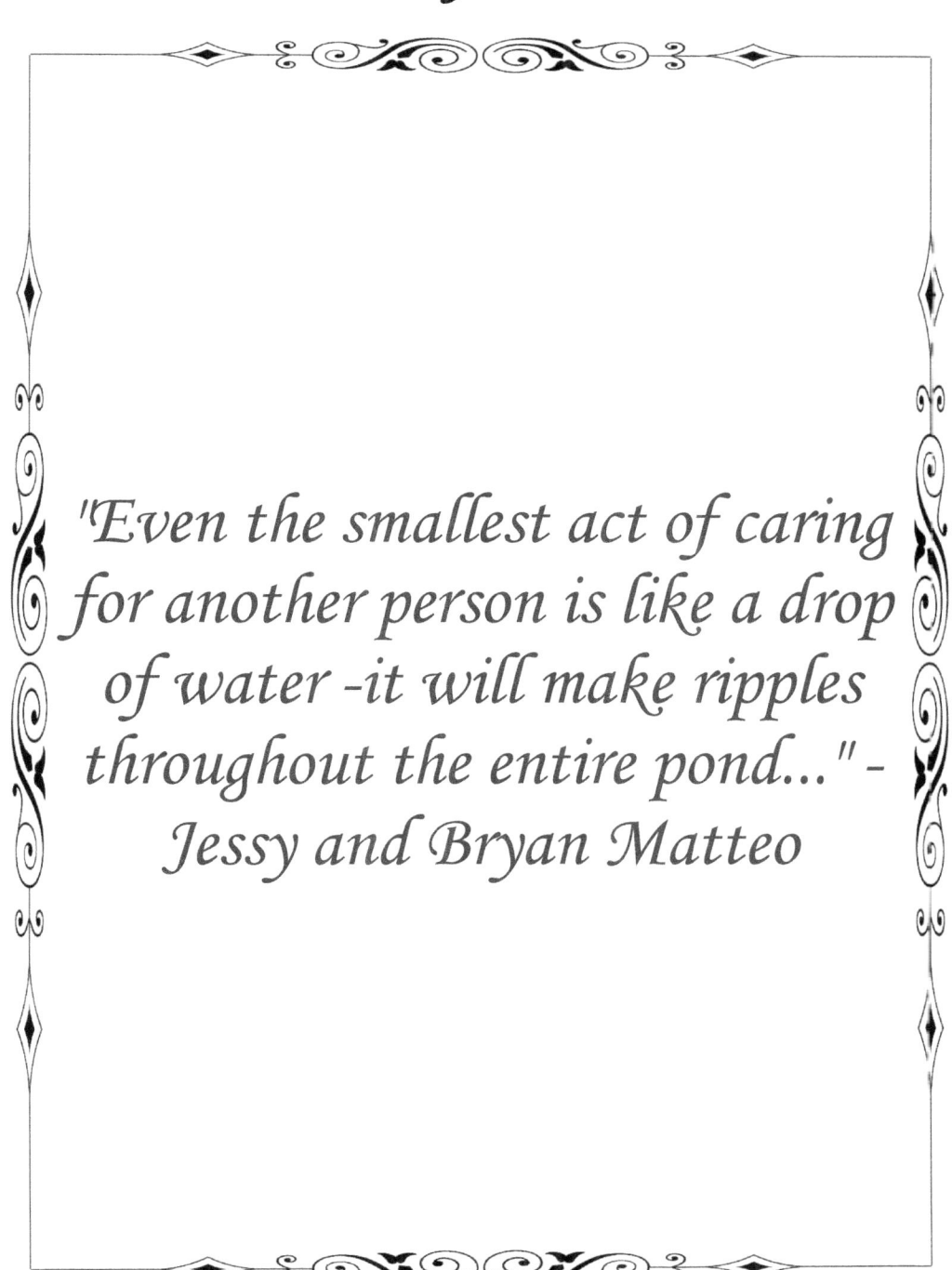

"Even the smallest act of caring for another person is like a drop of water -it will make ripples throughout the entire pond..." - Jessy and Bryan Matteo

Your Daily Motivational Quote
Day 225

"Success is stumbling from failure to failure with no loss of enthusiasm." -Winston Churchill

Your Daily Motivational Quote
Day 226

"Without a family, man, alone in the world, trembles with the cold." -Andre Maurois

Your Daily Motivational Quote
Day 227

"Strength does not come from physical capacity. It comes from an indomitable will." -Mahatma Gandhi

Your Daily Motivational Quote
Day 228

"Let no one ever come to you without leaving happier." - Mother Teresa

Your Daily Motivational Quote
Day 229

"The happiest people don't have the best of everything; they just make the best of everything." - unknown

Your Daily Motivational Quote
Day 230

"Learning how to love the little things in life is called learning how to be happy." -Marinela Reka

Your Daily Motivational Quote
Day 231

"Honesty is the first chapter in the book of wisdom." -Thomas Jefferson

Your Daily Motivational Quote
Day 232

"Yes, in all my research, the greatest leaders looked inward and were able to tell a good story with authenticity and passion." - Deepak Chopra

Your Daily Motivational Quote
Day 233

"I invite everyone to choose forgiveness rather than division, teamwork over personal ambition." -Jean-Francois Cope

Your Daily Motivational Quote
Day 234

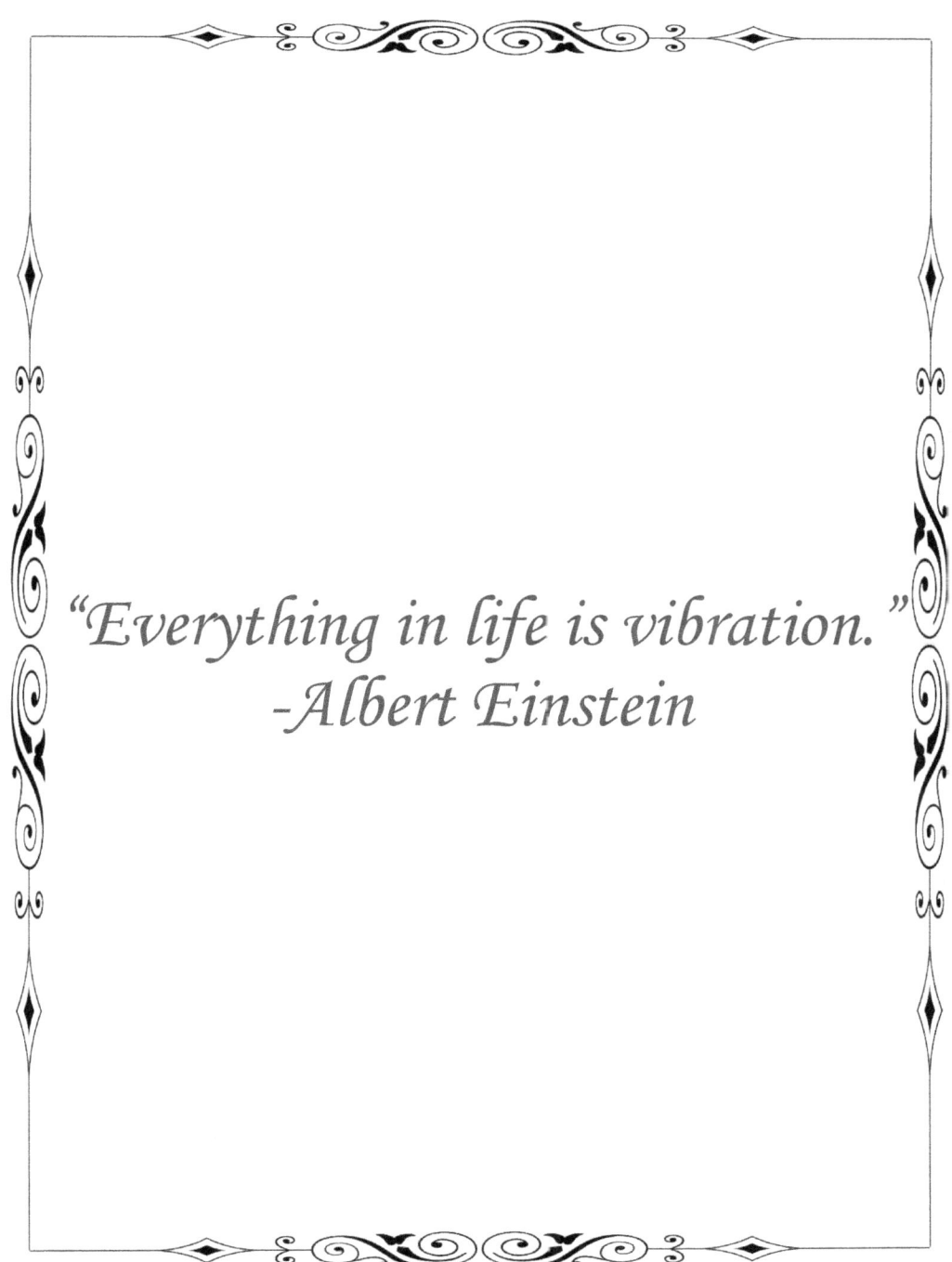

"Everything in life is vibration."
-Albert Einstein

Your Daily Motivational Quote
Day 235

"Life is far too important a thing ever to talk seriously about." - Oscar Wilde

Your Daily Motivational Quote
Day 236

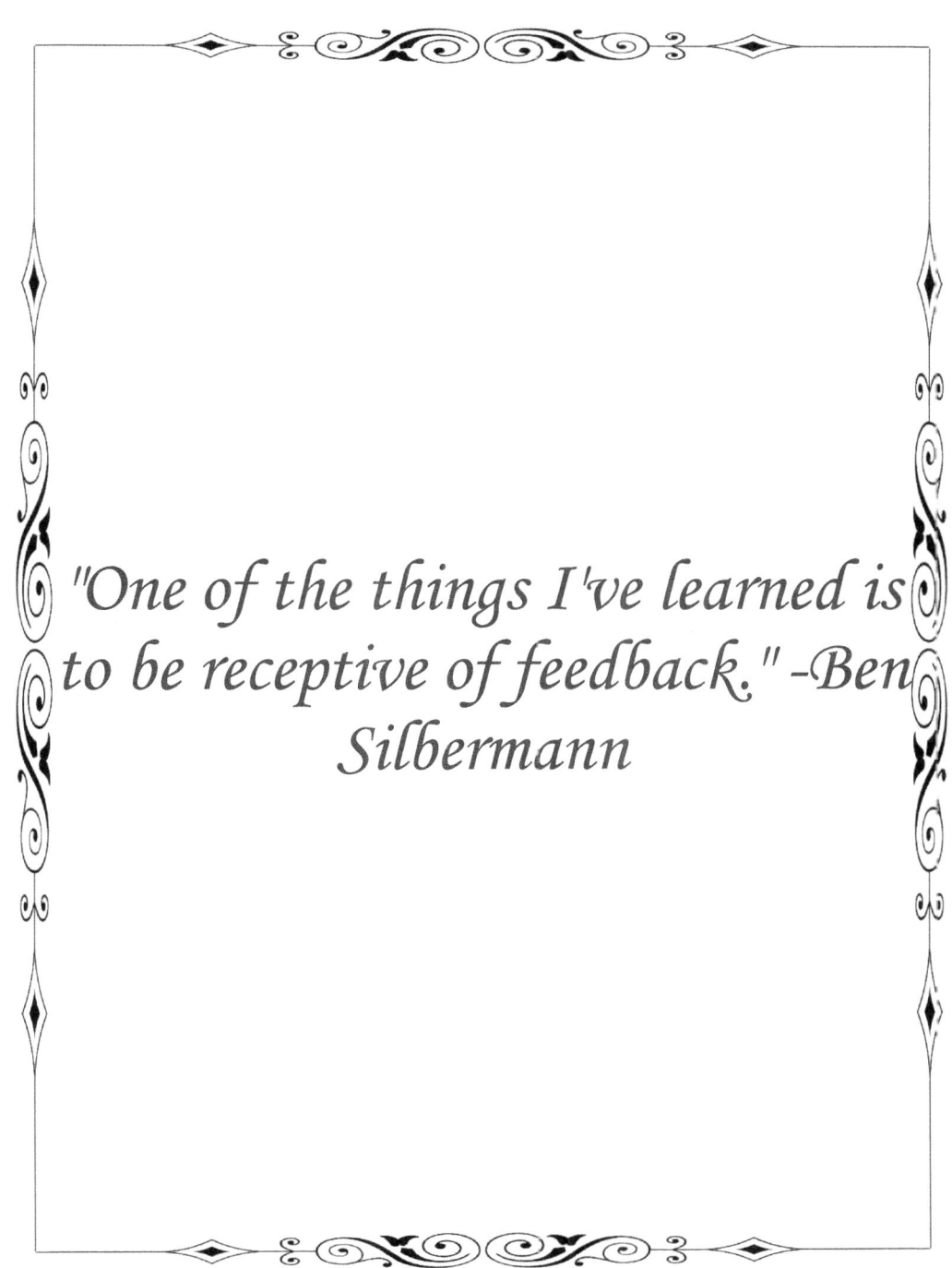

"One of the things I've learned is to be receptive of feedback." -Ben Silbermann

Your Daily Motivational Quote
Day 237

"A wise man adapts himself to circumstances, as water shapes itself to the vessel that contains it." -Chinese Proverb

Your Daily Motivational Quote
Day 238

"You can't fake passion." - Barbara Corcoran

Your Daily Motivational Quote
Day 239

"The family is one of nature's masterpieces." -George Santayana

Your Daily Motivational Quote
Day 240

"True forgiveness is when you can say, "Thank you for that experience." -Oprah Winfrey

Your Daily Motivational Quote
Day 241

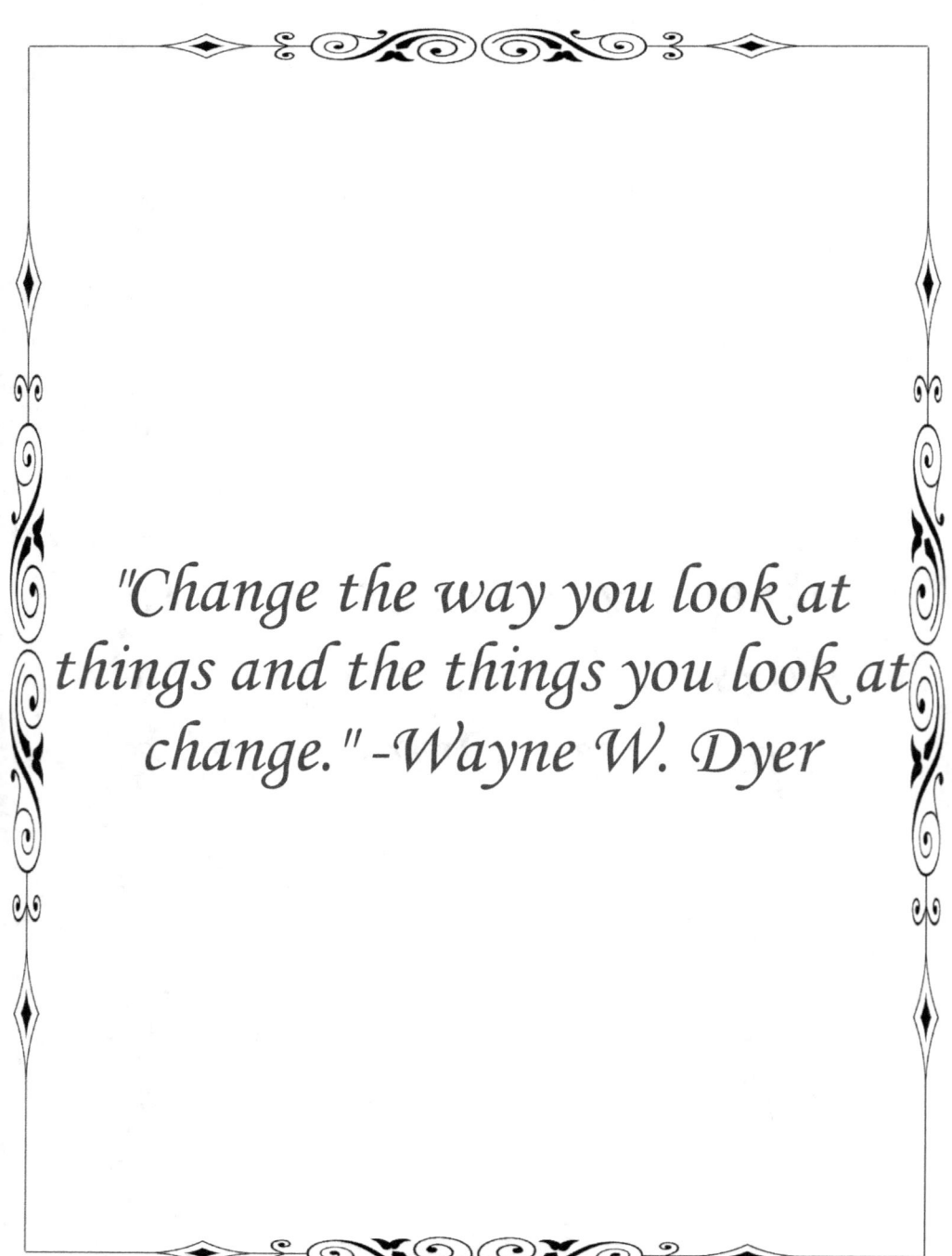

"Change the way you look at things and the things you look at change." -Wayne W. Dyer

Your Daily Motivational Quote
Day 242

"Trust yourself. Then you will know how to live." -Johann Wolfgang von Goethe

Your Daily Motivational Quote
Day 243

"Innovation distinguishes between a leader and a follower."
-Steve Jobs

Your Daily Motivational Quote
Day 244

"Don't cross the bridge until you come to it." -proverb

Your Daily Motivational Quote
Day 245

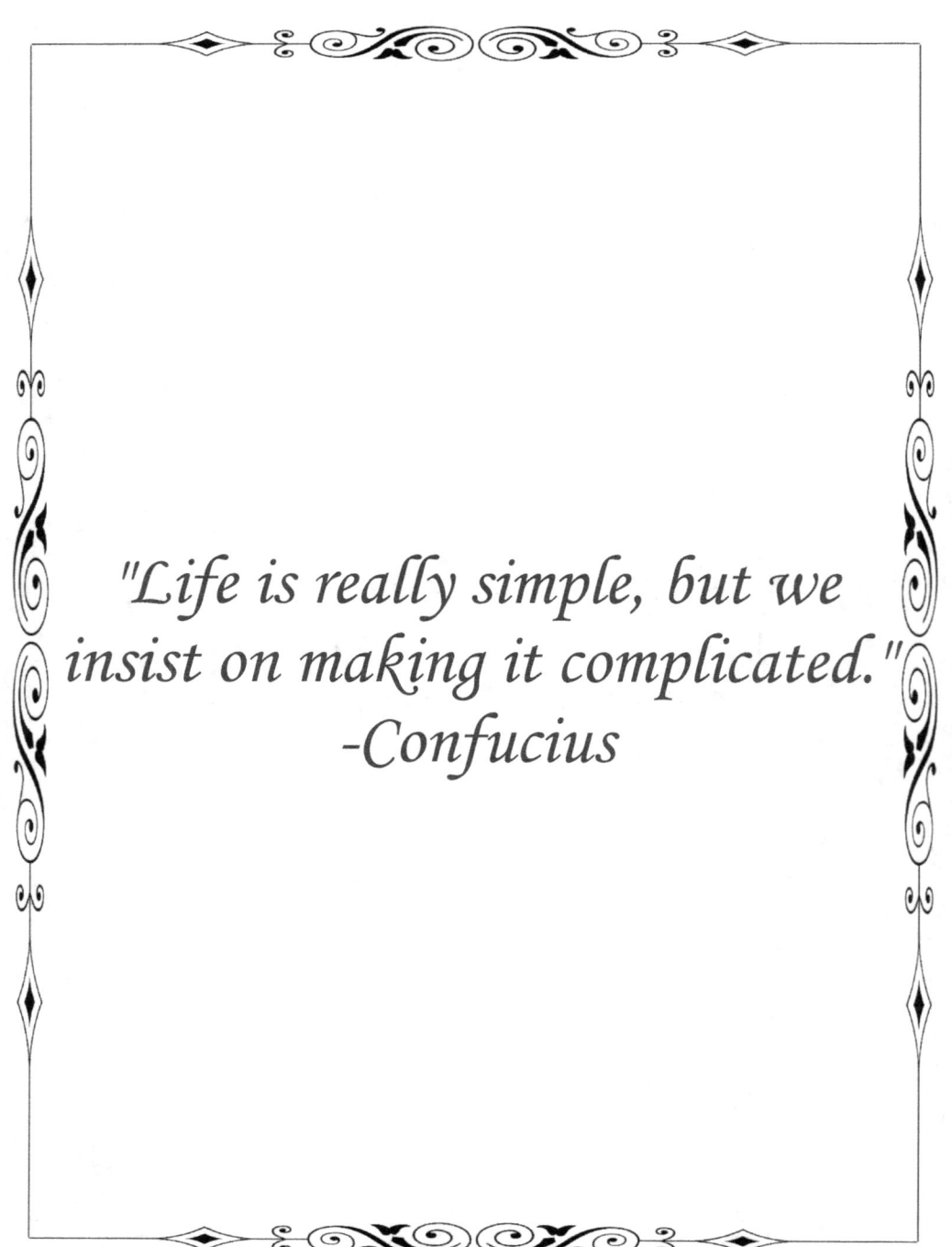

"Life is really simple, but we insist on making it complicated."
-Confucius

Your Daily Motivational Quote
Day 246

"Nothing is impossible, the word itself says 'I'm possible'!" - Audrey Hepburn

Your Daily Motivational Quote
Day 247

"It's nice to be important, but it's important to be nice." - Kermit the Frog

Your Daily Motivational Quote
Day 248

"The bad news is time flies. The good news is you're the pilot." - Michael Althsuler

Your Daily Motivational Quote
Day 249

"Whenever you find yourself doubting how far you can go, just remember how far you have come. Remember everything you have faced, all the battles you have won, and all the fears you have overcome." -unknown

Your Daily Motivational Quote
Day 250

"A kind gesture can reach a wound that only compassion can heal." -Steve Maraboli

Your Daily Motivational Quote
Day 251

"You are never too old to set another goal or dream a new dream." -C.S. Lewis

Your Daily Motivational Quote
Day 252

"I love when things are transparent, free and clear of all inhibition and judgment." - Pharrell Williams

Your Daily Motivational Quote
Day 253

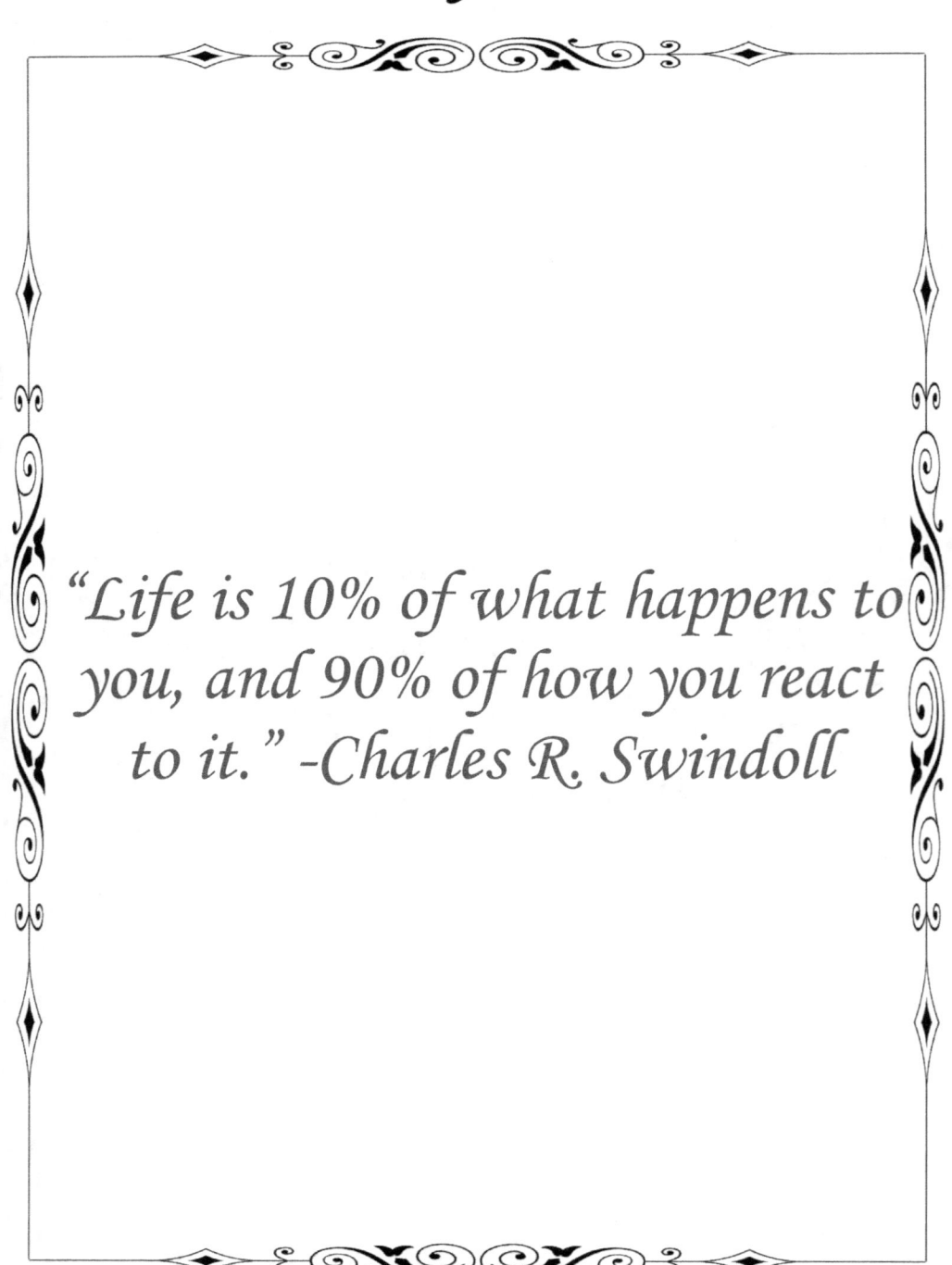

"Life is 10% of what happens to you, and 90% of how you react to it." -Charles R. Swindoll

Your Daily Motivational Quote
Day 254

"The best way to have a good idea is to have lots of ideas." - Linus Pauling

Your Daily Motivational Quote
Day 255

"Life is a play. It's not its length, but its performance that counts." -Seneca

Your Daily Motivational Quote
Day 256

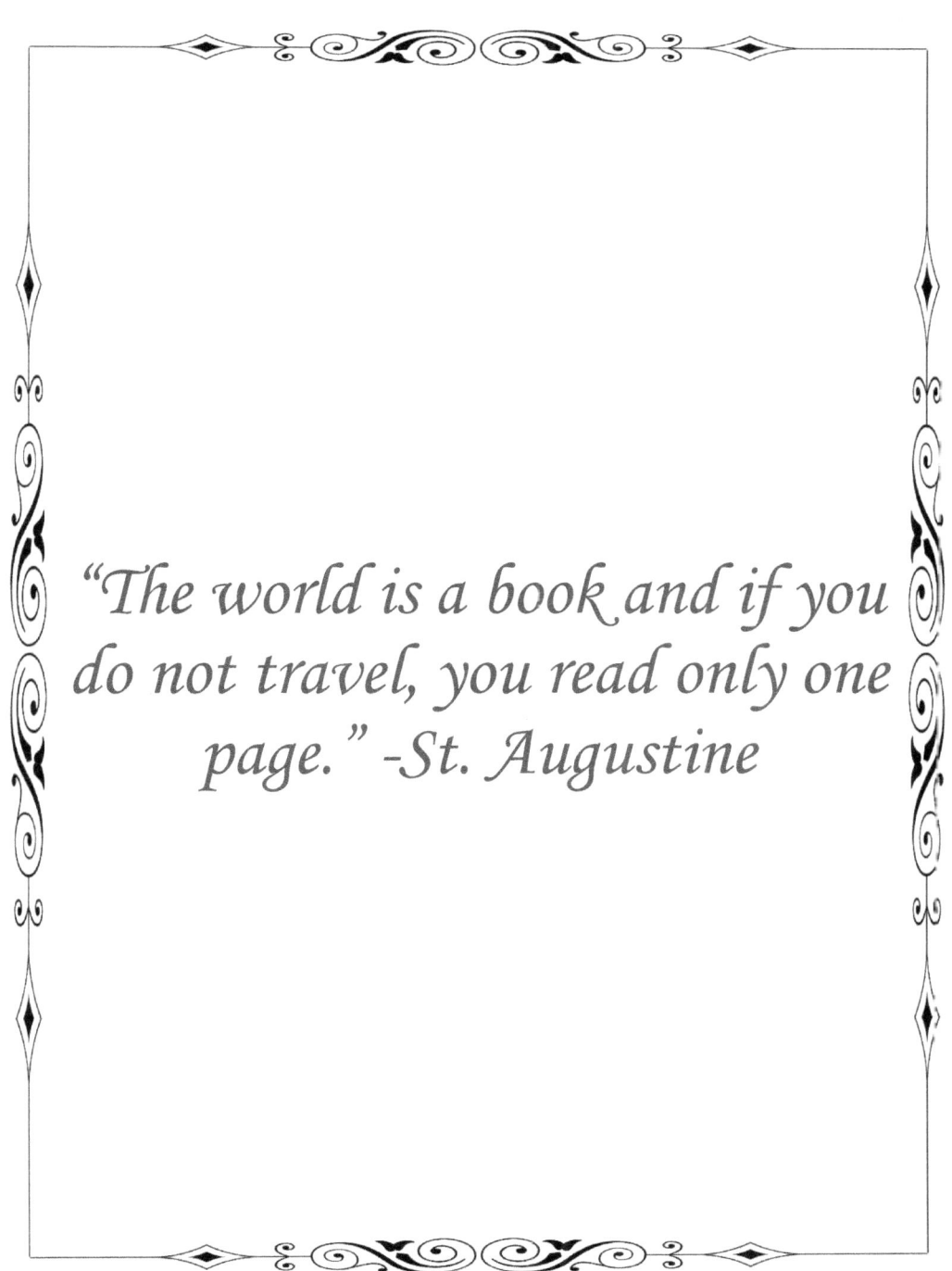

"The world is a book and if you do not travel, you read only one page." -St. Augustine

Your Daily Motivational Quote
Day 257

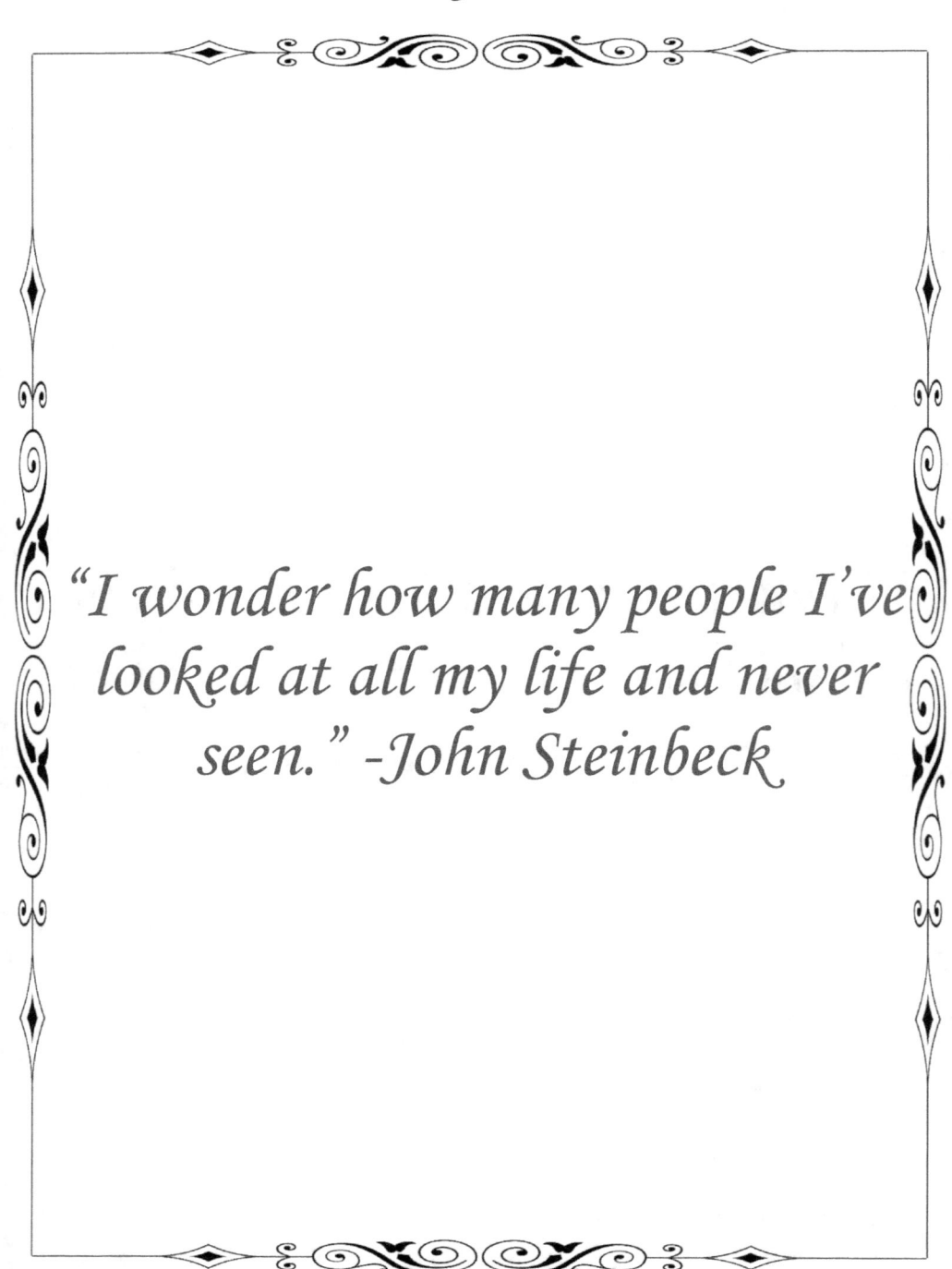

"I wonder how many people I've looked at all my life and never seen." -John Steinbeck

Your Daily Motivational Quote
Day 258

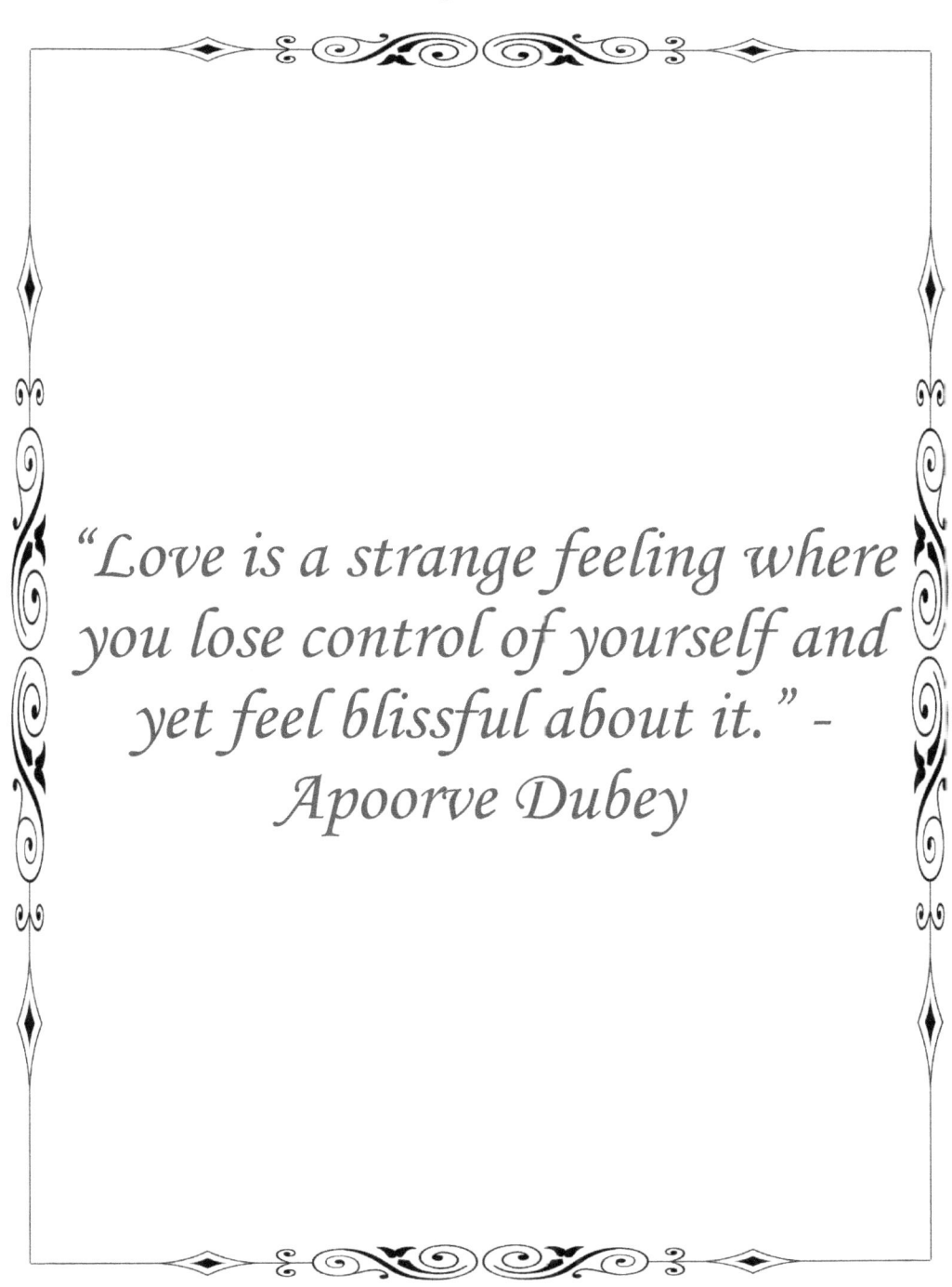

"Love is a strange feeling where you lose control of yourself and yet feel blissful about it." - Apoorve Dubey

Your Daily Motivational Quote
Day 259

"To the world, you may be one person; but to one person, you may be the world." -Dr. Seuss

Your Daily Motivational Quote
Day 260

"Life belongs to the living, and he who lives must be prepared for changes" -Johann Wolfgang von Goethe

Your Daily Motivational Quote
Day 261

"Some people feel the rain. Others just get wet." -Bob Marley

Your Daily Motivational Quote
Day 262

"Smile, it lets your teeth breathe!" -unknown

Your Daily Motivational Quote
Day 263

"Simplicity is not the goal. It is the by-product of a good idea and modest expectations." -Paul Rand

Your Daily Motivational Quote
Day 264

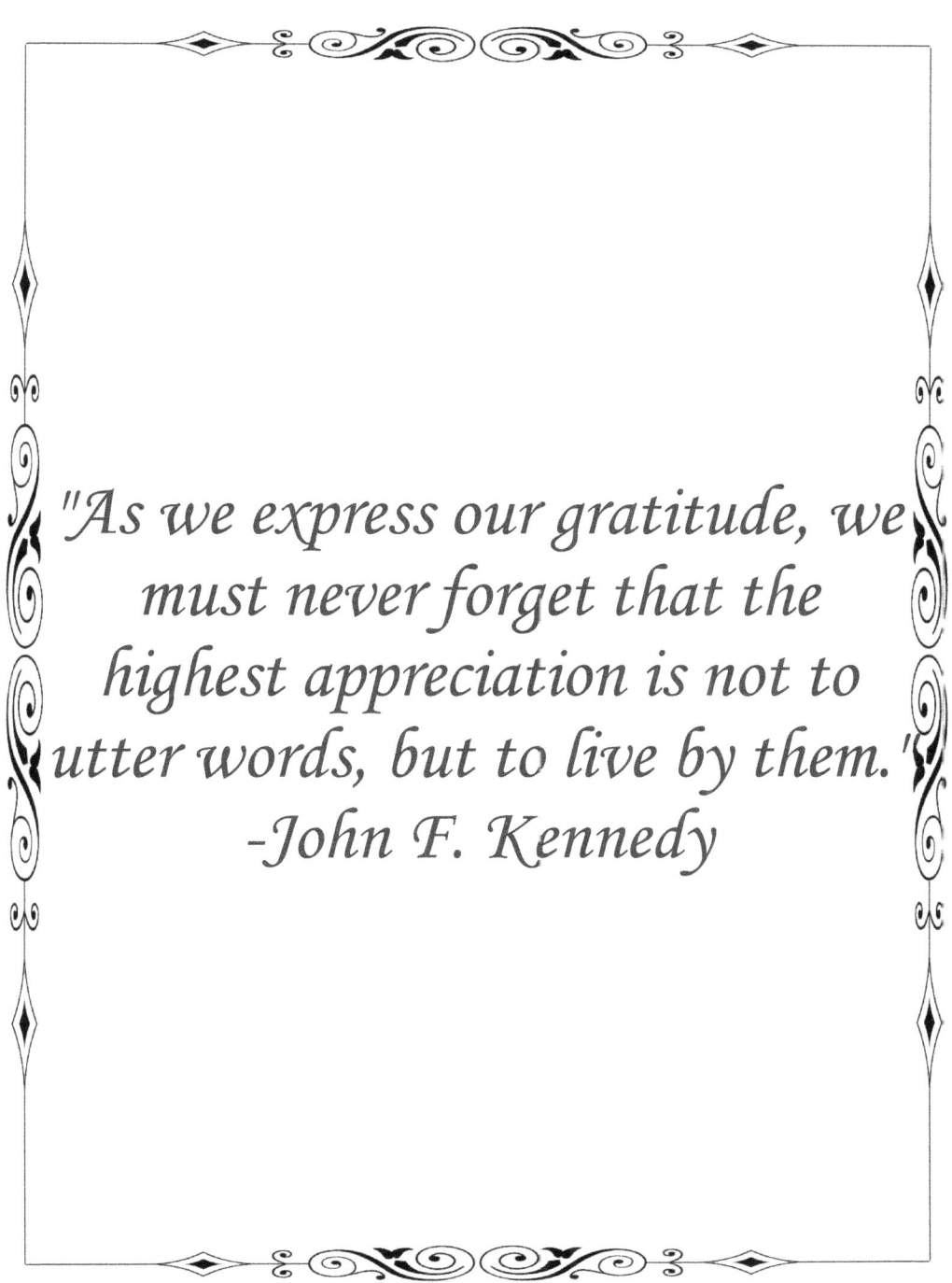

"As we express our gratitude, we must never forget that the highest appreciation is not to utter words, but to live by them."
-John F. Kennedy

Your Daily Motivational Quote
Day 265

"If everyone is moving forward together, then success takes care of itself." -Henry Ford

Your Daily Motivational Quote
Day 266

"Fall seven times and stand up eight." -Japanese Proverb

Your Daily Motivational Quote
Day 267

"The most important thing is to enjoy your life – to be happy – it's all that matters." -Audrey Hepburn

Your Daily Motivational Quote
Day 268

"Do not spoil what you have by desiring what you have not; remember that what you now have was once among the things you only hoped for." -Epicurus

Your Daily Motivational Quote
Day 269

"The smallest act of kindness is worth more than the greatest intention." -Kahlil Gibran

Your Daily Motivational Quote
Day 270

"Being happy never goes out of style." -Lilly Pulitzer

Your Daily Motivational Quote
Day 271

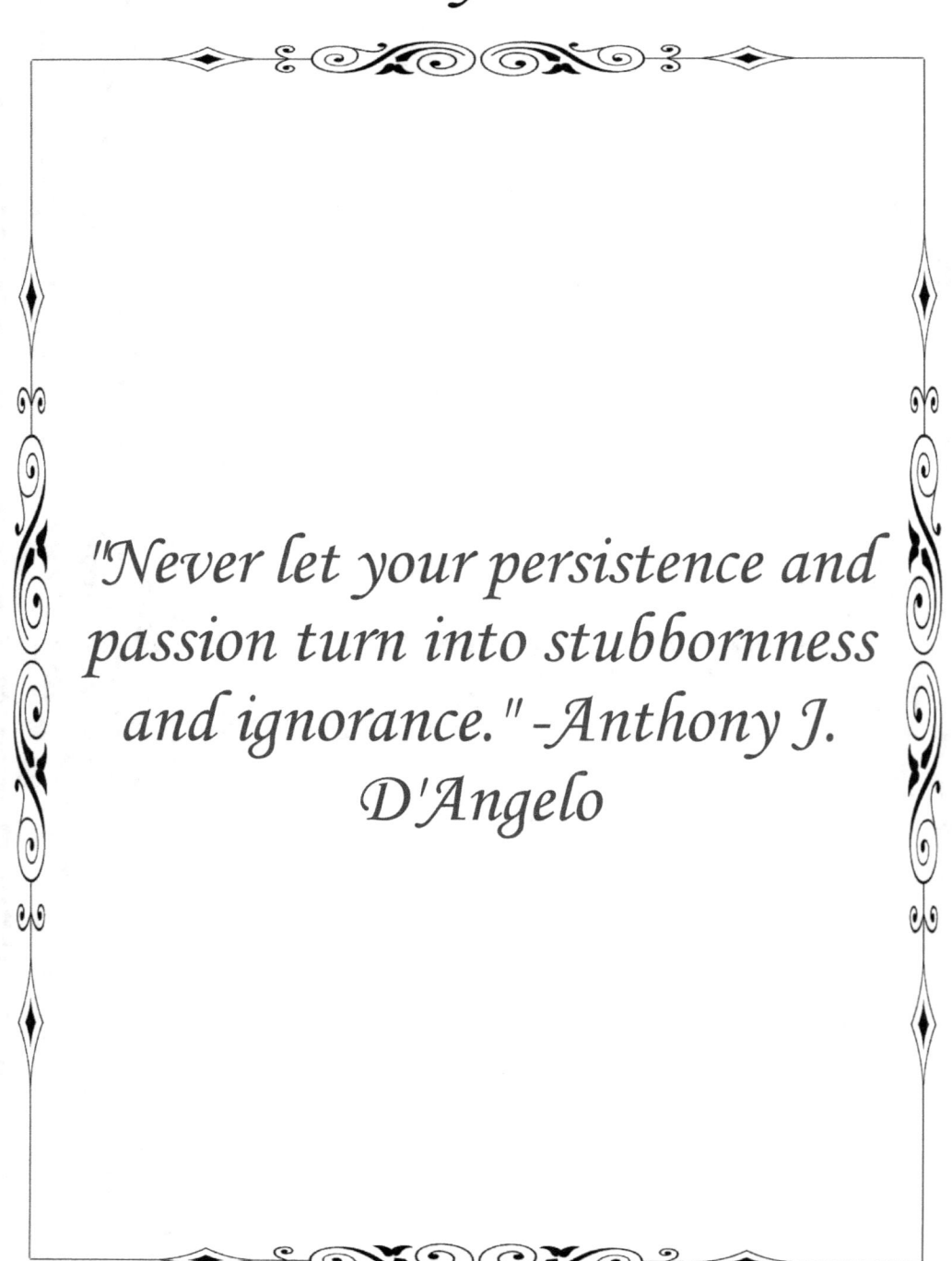

"Never let your persistence and passion turn into stubbornness and ignorance." -Anthony J. D'Angelo

Your Daily Motivational Quote
Day 272

"What we spend, we lose. What we keep will be left for others. What we give away will be ours forever." -David McGee

Your Daily Motivational Quote
Day 273

"We gain strength, and courage, and confidence by each experience in which we really stop to look fear in the face... we must do that which we think we cannot." -Eleanor Roosevelt

Your Daily Motivational Quote
Day 274

"Dream big, work hard, and don't be an asshole." -Mike Shinoda

Your Daily Motivational Quote
Day 275

"There is no greatness where there is no simplicity, goodness and truth." -Leo Tolstoy

Your Daily Motivational Quote
Day 276

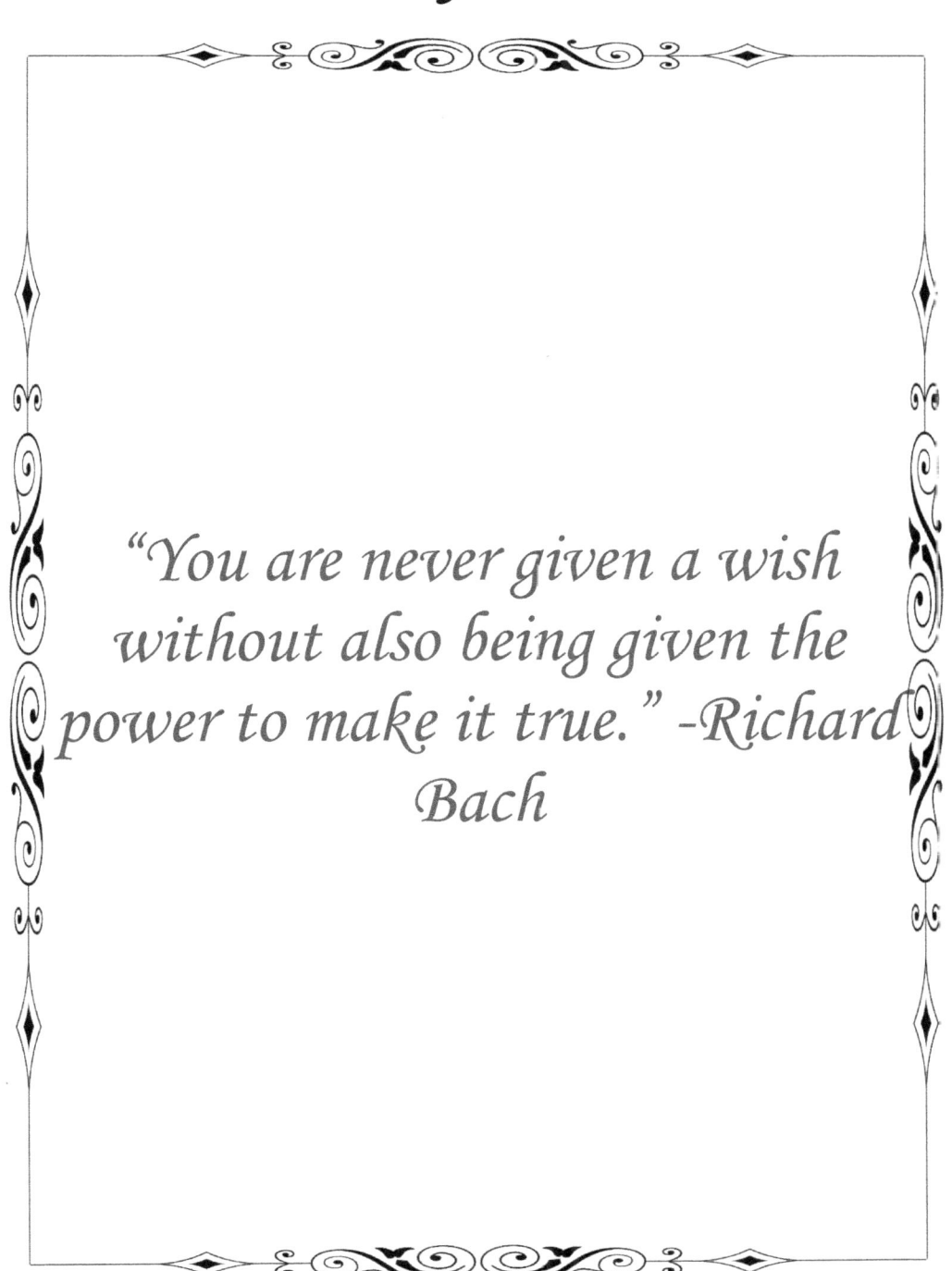

"You are never given a wish without also being given the power to make it true." -Richard Bach

Your Daily Motivational Quote
Day 277

"She's a dreamer, a doer, a thinker. She sees possibility everywhere." -unknown

Your Daily Motivational Quote
Day 278

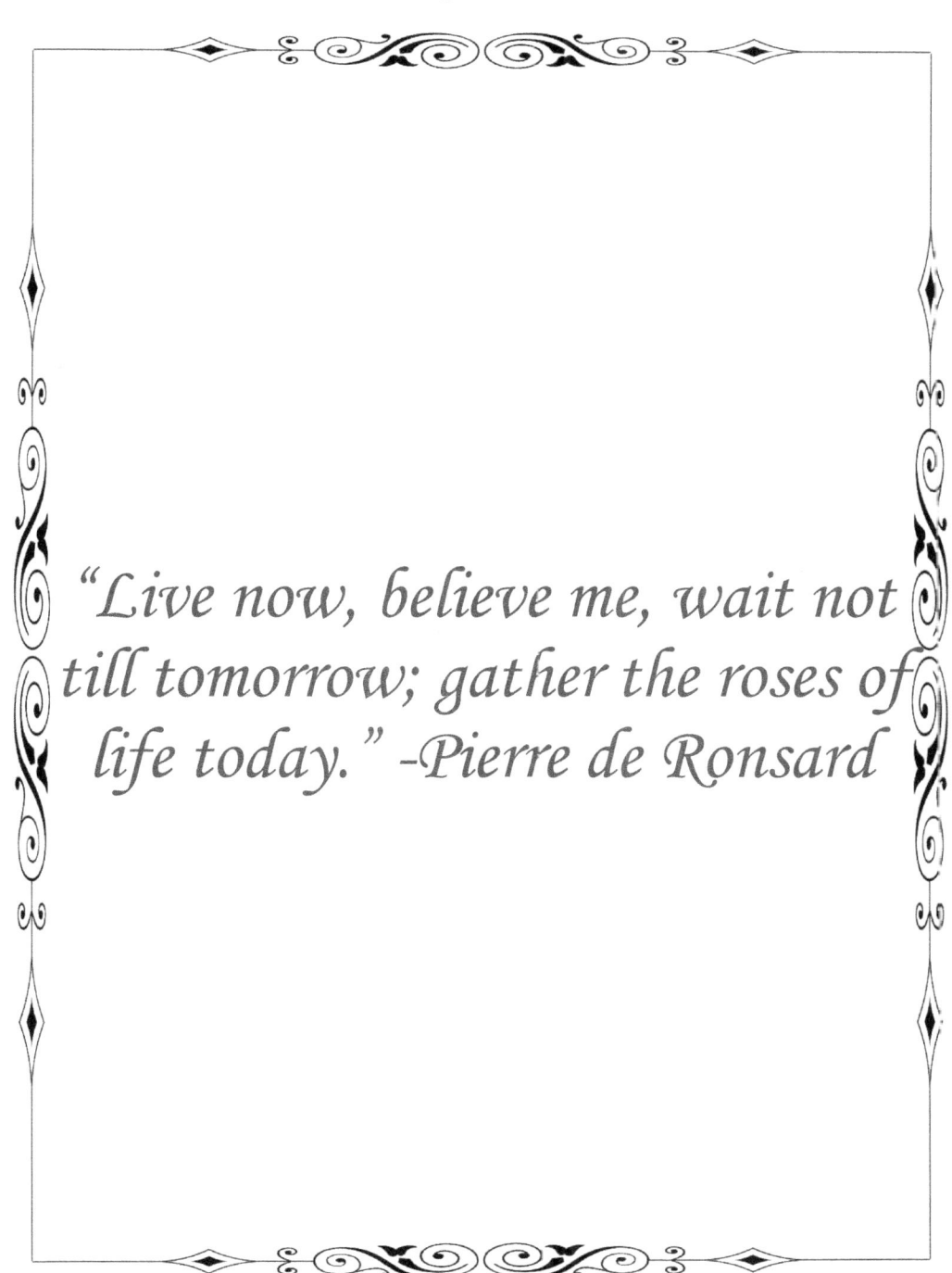

"Live now, believe me, wait not till tomorrow; gather the roses of life today." -Pierre de Ronsard

Your Daily Motivational Quote
Day 279

"I do not try to dance better than anyone else. I only try to dance better than myself." - Mikhail Baryshnikov

Your Daily Motivational Quote
Day 280

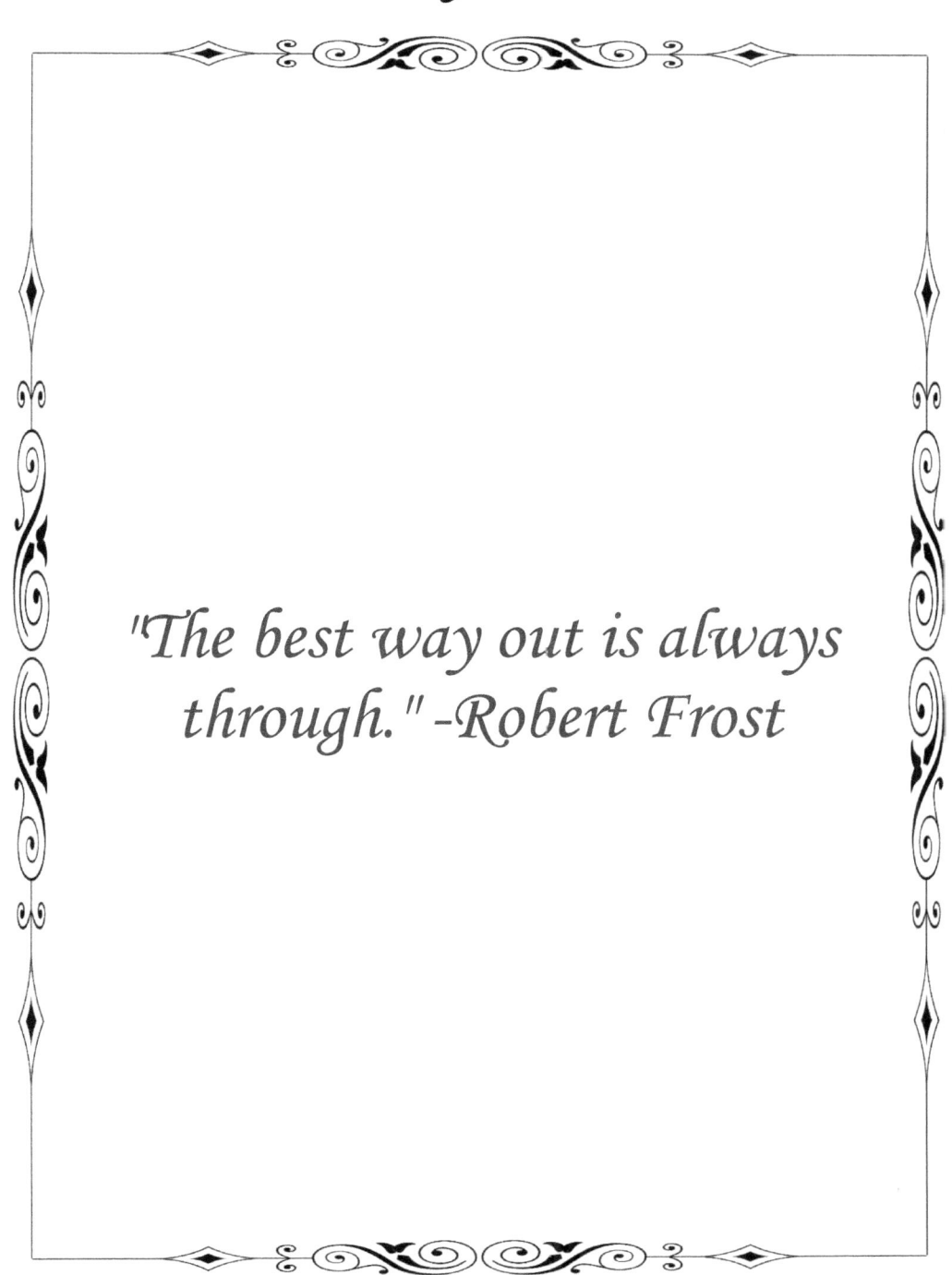

"The best way out is always through." -Robert Frost

Your Daily Motivational Quote
Day 281

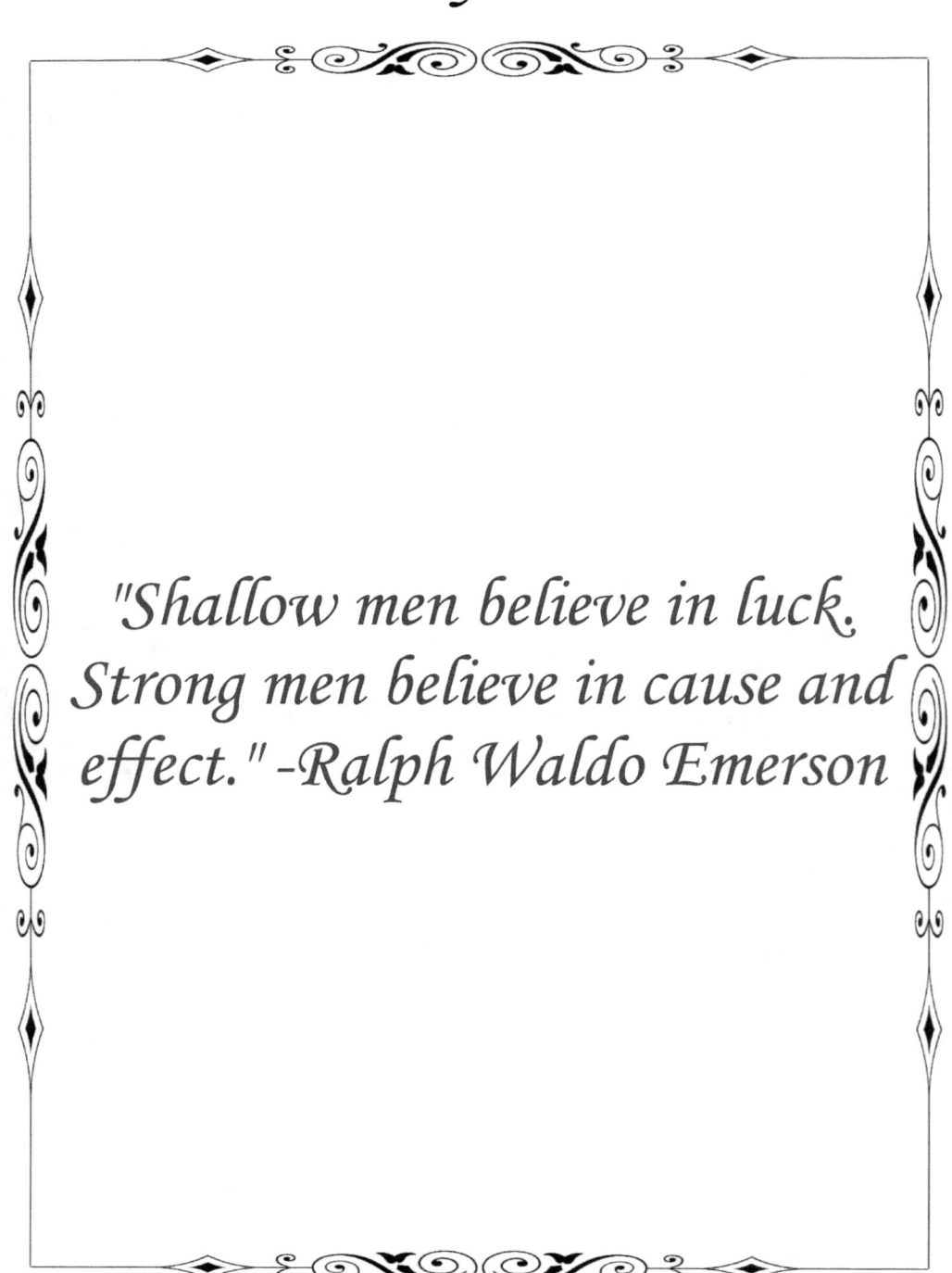

"Shallow men believe in luck. Strong men believe in cause and effect." -Ralph Waldo Emerson

Your Daily Motivational Quote
Day 282

"You can't buy happiness but you can buy a lift pass." - unknown

Your Daily Motivational Quote
Day 283

"Sometimes the heart knows things the mind could never explain." -Ranjeet

Your Daily Motivational Quote
Day 284

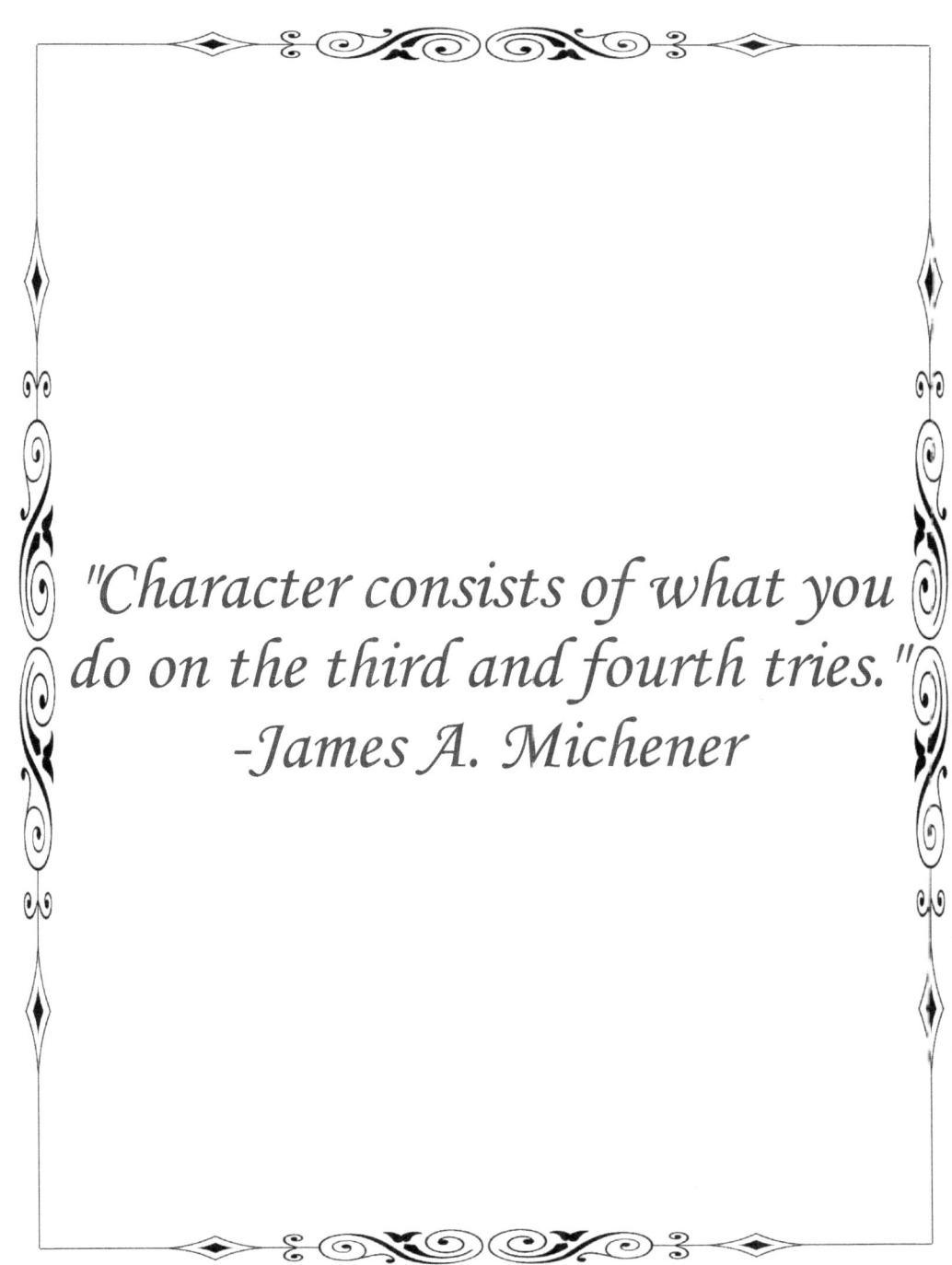

"Character consists of what you do on the third and fourth tries."
-James A. Michener

Your Daily Motivational Quote
Day 285

"No one has ever become poor by giving." -Anne Frank

Your Daily Motivational Quote
Day 286

"The optimist sees the rose and not its thorns; the pessimist stares at the thorns, oblivious to the rose." -Kahlil Gibran

Your Daily Motivational Quote
Day 287

"We are shaped and fashioned by what we love." -Goethe

Your Daily Motivational Quote
Day 288

"We're all working together; that's the secret." -Sam Walton

Your Daily Motivational Quote
Day 289

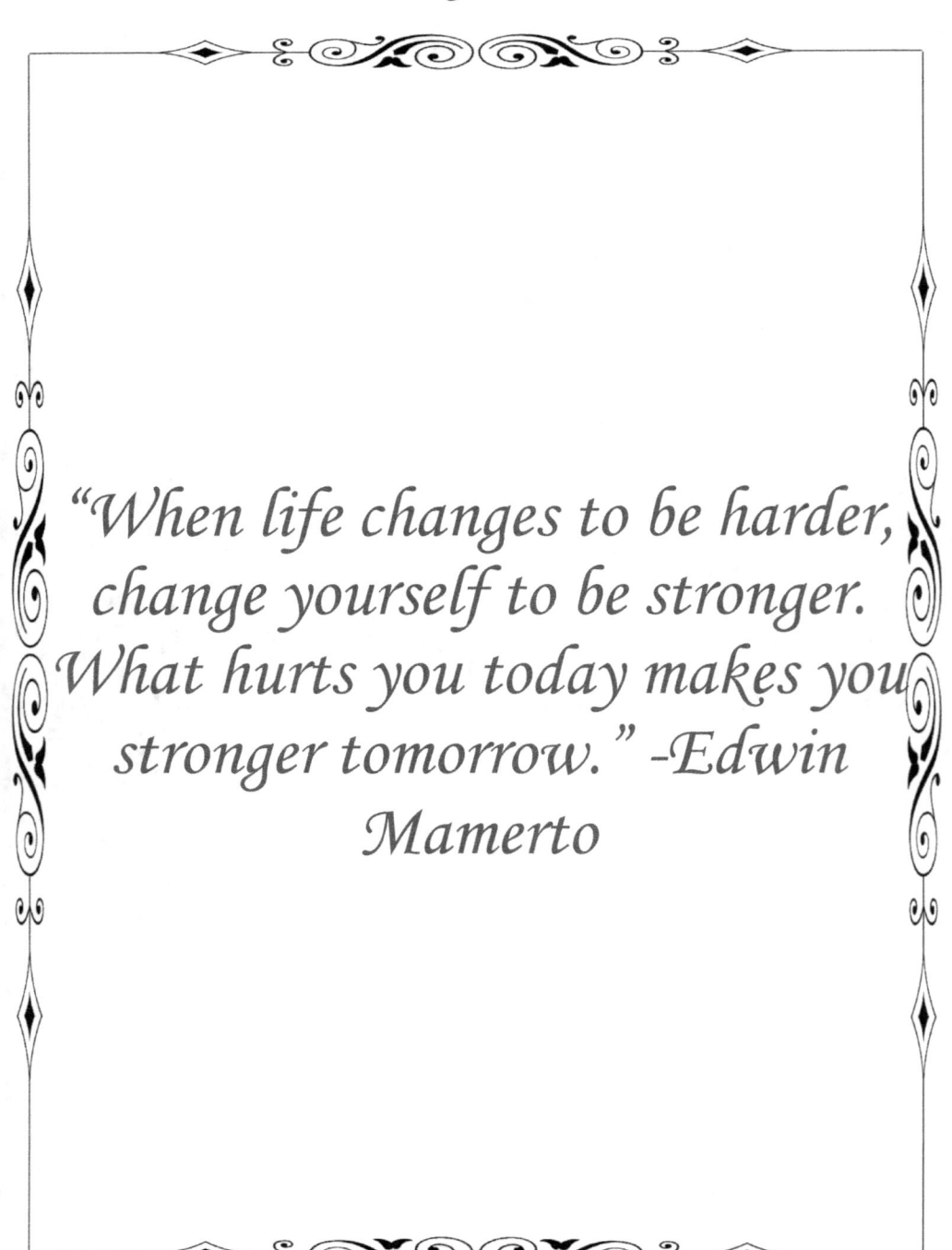

"When life changes to be harder, change yourself to be stronger. What hurts you today makes you stronger tomorrow." -Edwin Mamerto

Your Daily Motivational Quote
Day 290

"You're never too old to do goofy stuff." -Ward Cleaver

Your Daily Motivational Quote
Day 291

"Courage is the most important of all the virtues because without courage, you can't practice any other virtue consistently." -Maya Angelou

Your Daily Motivational Quote
Day 292

"Tomorrow we will do beautiful things." -Antoni Gaudi

Your Daily Motivational Quote
Day 293

"Don't forget: beautiful sunsets need cloudy skies." -Paulo Coelho

Your Daily Motivational Quote
Day 294

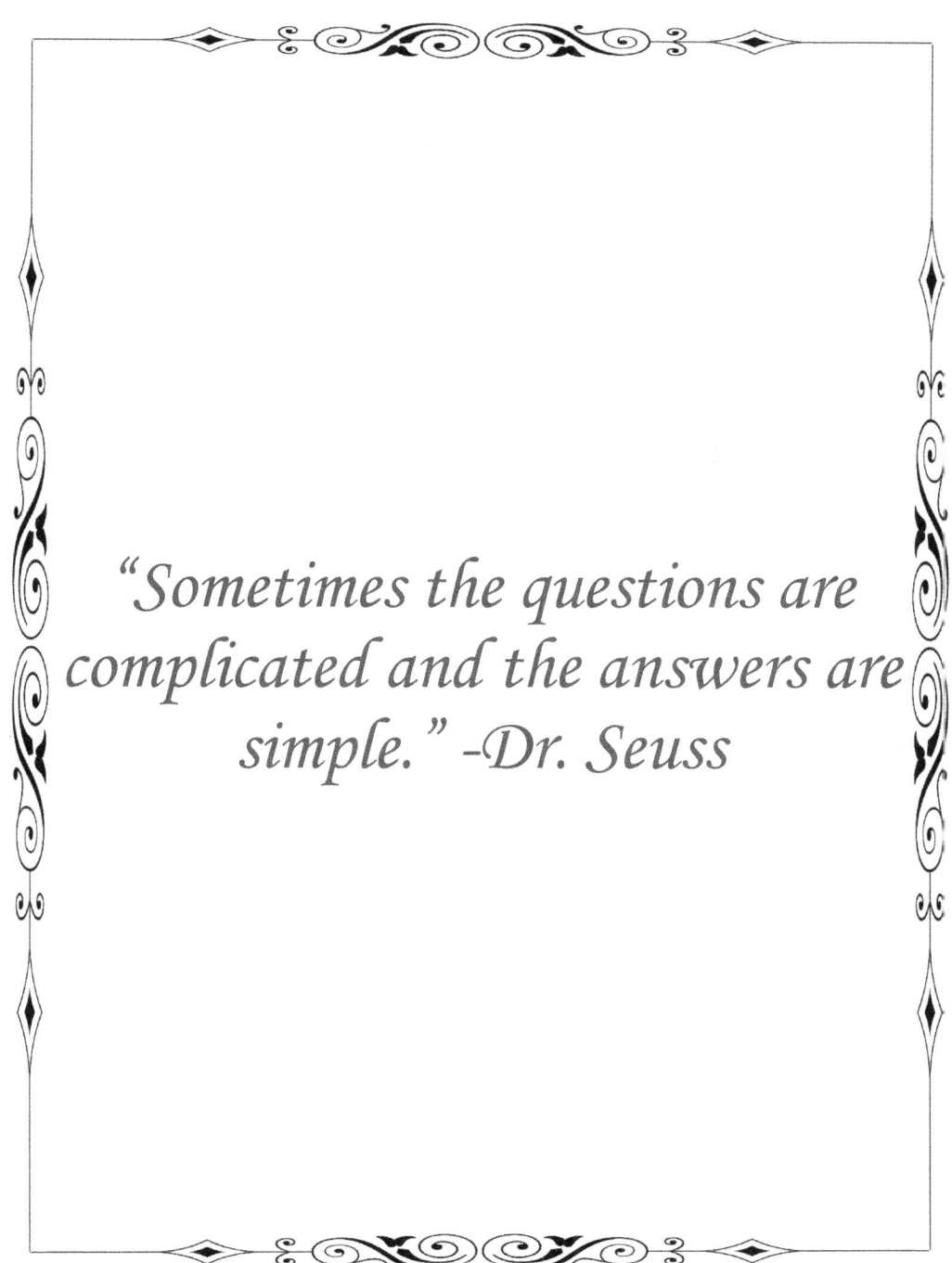

"Sometimes the questions are complicated and the answers are simple." -Dr. Seuss

Your Daily Motivational Quote
Day 295

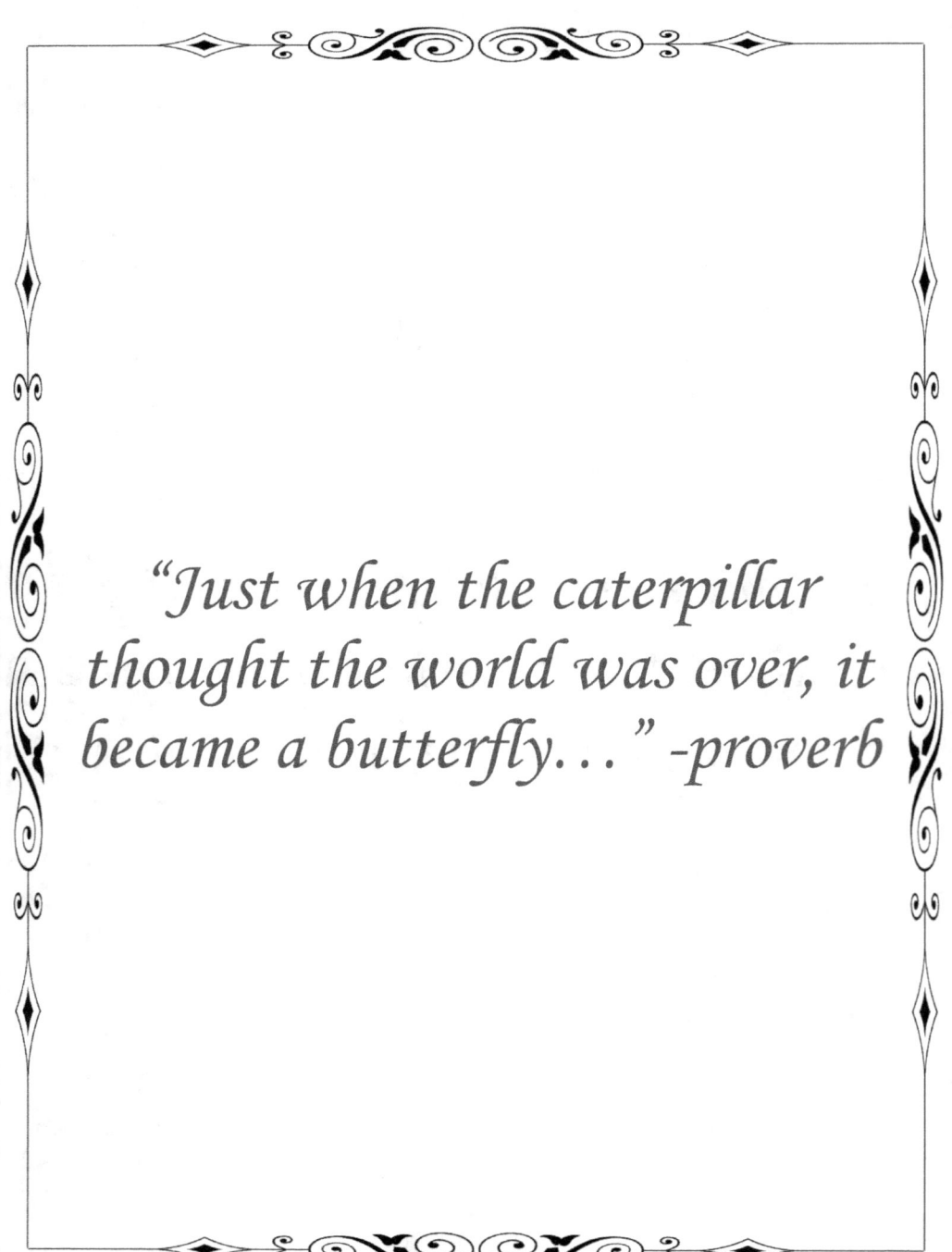

"Just when the caterpillar thought the world was over, it became a butterfly..." -proverb

Your Daily Motivational Quote
Day 296

"Act as if what you do makes a difference. It does." -William James

Your Daily Motivational Quote
Day 297

"It's kind of fun to do the impossible." -Walt E. Disney

Your Daily Motivational Quote
Day 298

"We must find time to stop and thank the people who make a difference in our lives." -John F. Kennedy

Your Daily Motivational Quote
Day 299

"That which does not kill us makes us stronger." -Friedrich Nietzsche

Your Daily Motivational Quote
Day 300

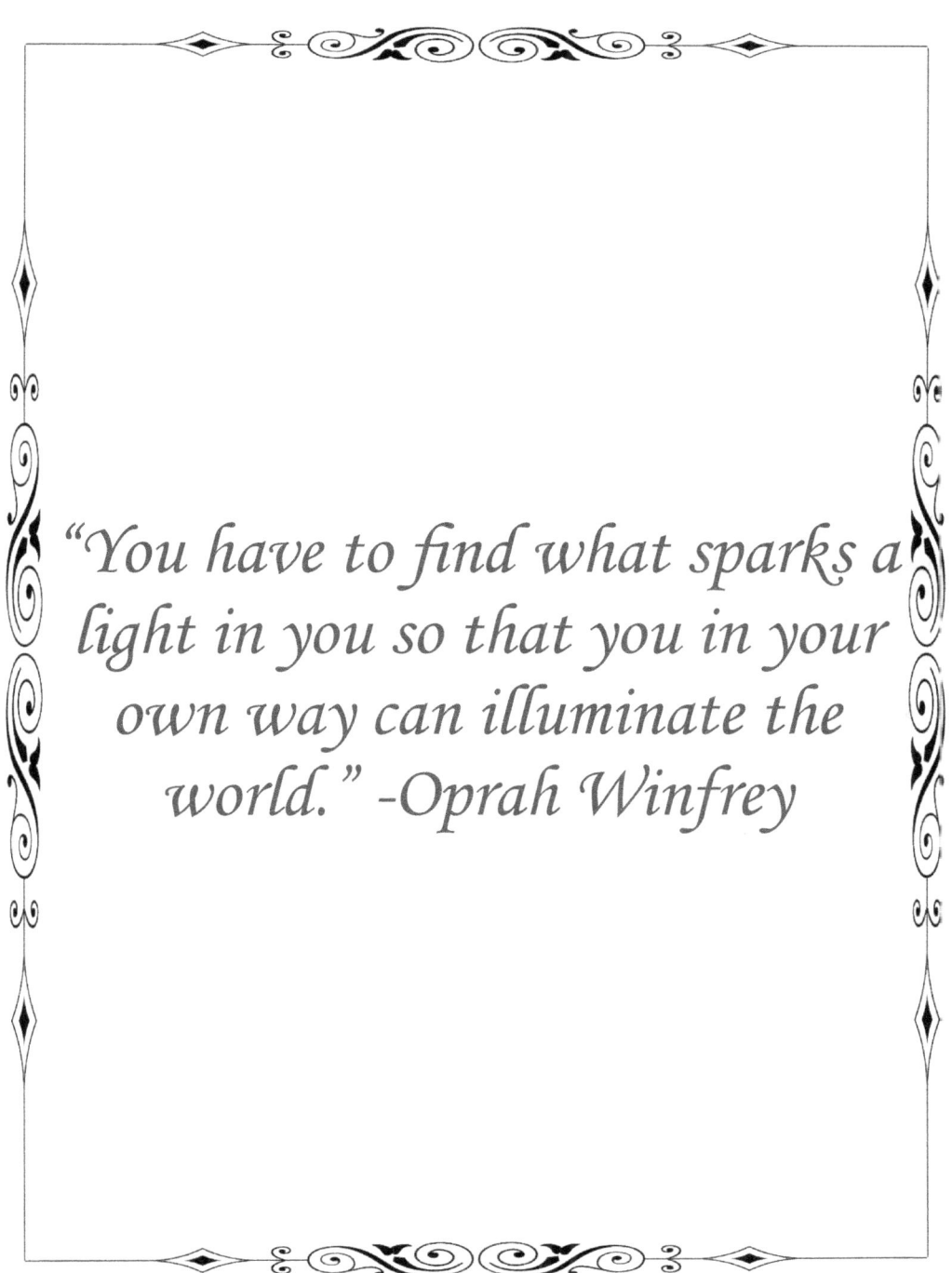

"You have to find what sparks a light in you so that you in your own way can illuminate the world." -Oprah Winfrey

Your Daily Motivational Quote
Day 301

"You can change the entire mood with lighting." -Karen Cobb

Your Daily Motivational Quote
Day 302

"Somewhere something incredible is waiting to be known." -Carl Sagan

Your Daily Motivational Quote
Day 303

"What I am looking for is not 'out there.' It is in me." -Helen Keller

Your Daily Motivational Quote
Day 304

"Magic is believing in yourself. If you can do that, you can make anything happen." -Goethe

Your Daily Motivational Quote
Day 305

"It's all about finding the calm in the chaos." -Donna Karan

Your Daily Motivational Quote
Day 306

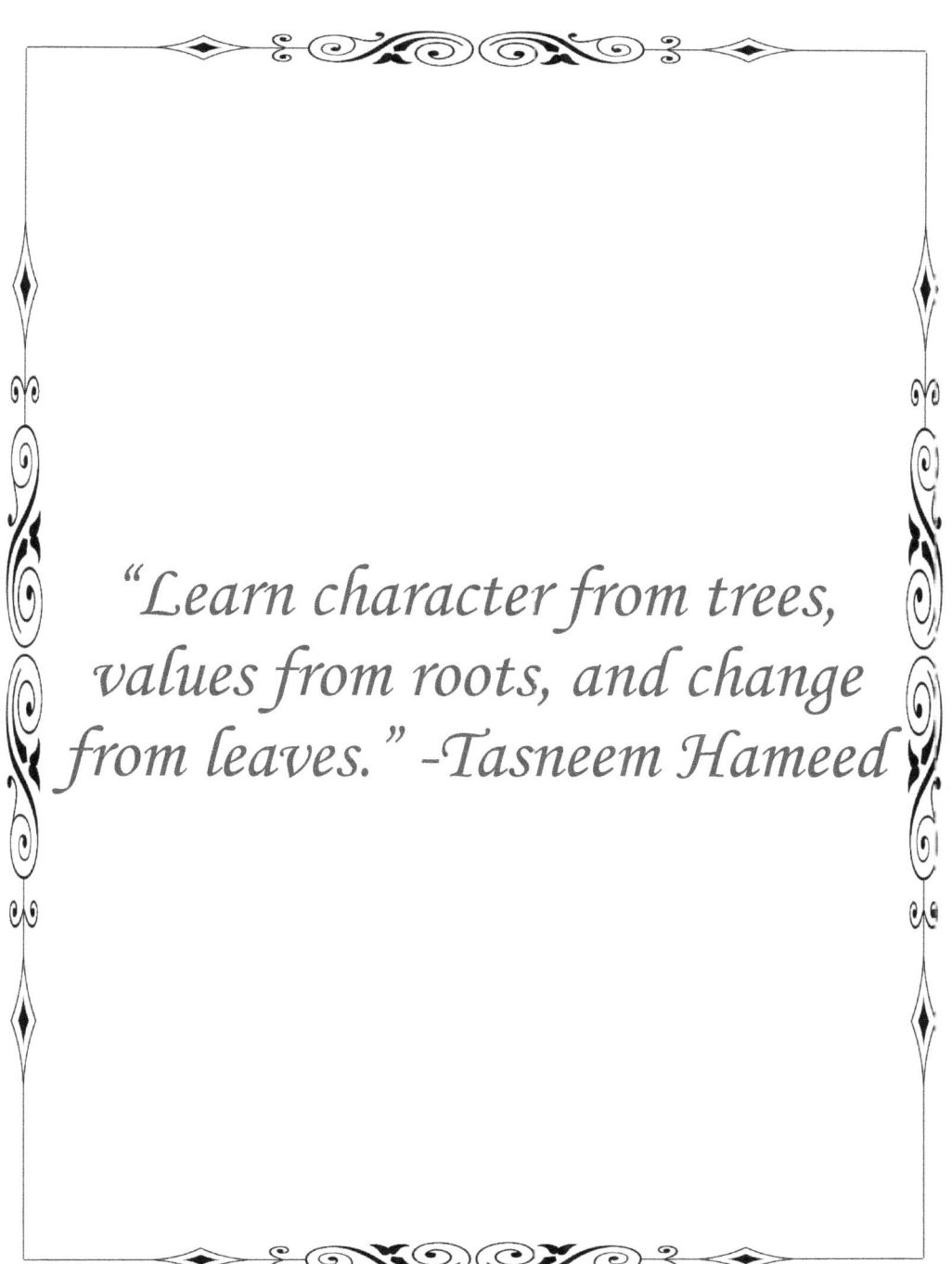

"Learn character from trees, values from roots, and change from leaves." -Tasneem Hameed

Your Daily Motivational Quote
Day 307

"Make subtlety obvious." -Billy Wilder

Your Daily Motivational Quote
Day 308

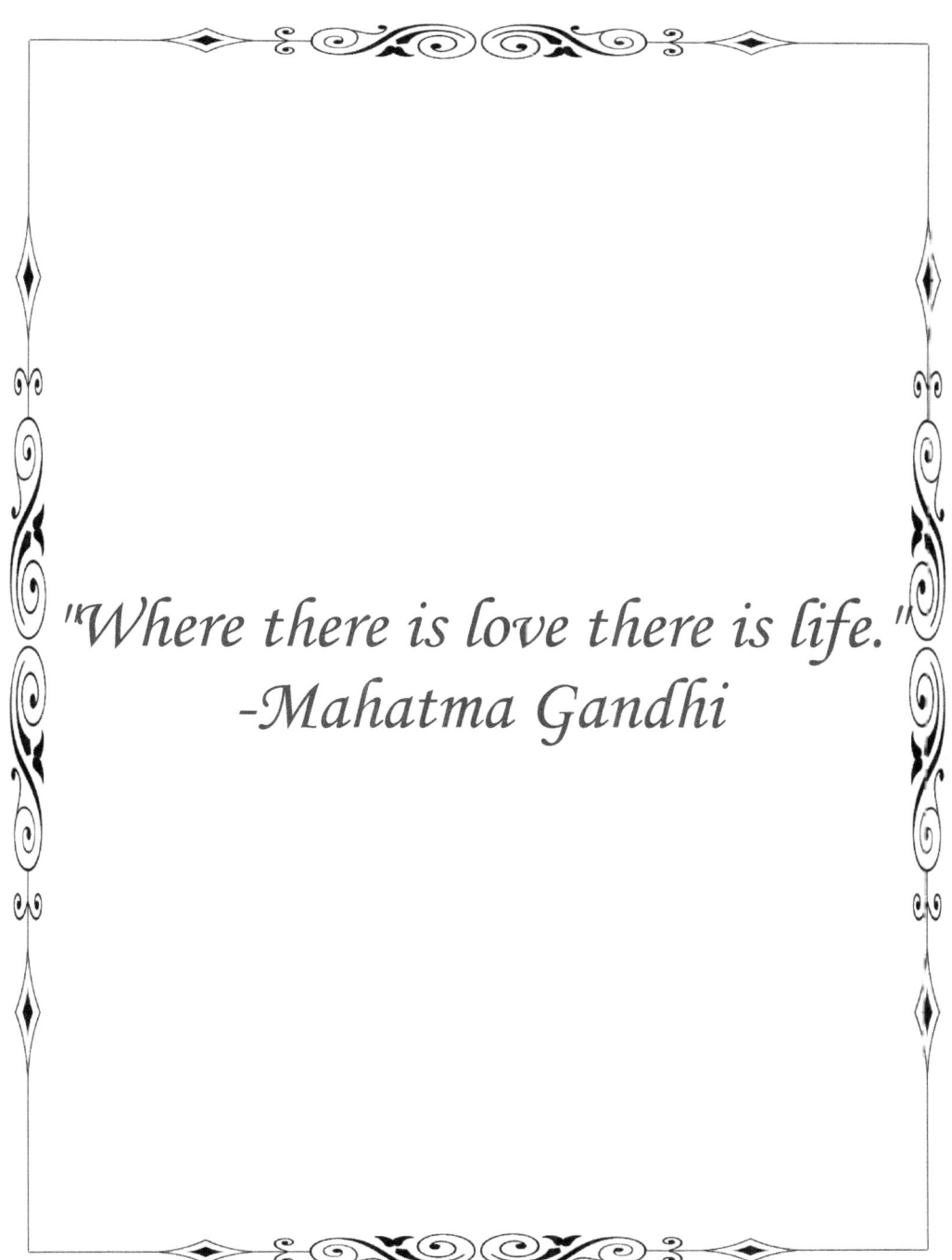

"Where there is love there is life."
-Mahatma Gandhi

Your Daily Motivational Quote
Day 309

"You do not exist to please someone else… you exist for your own sake." -Hank Green

Your Daily Motivational Quote
Day 310

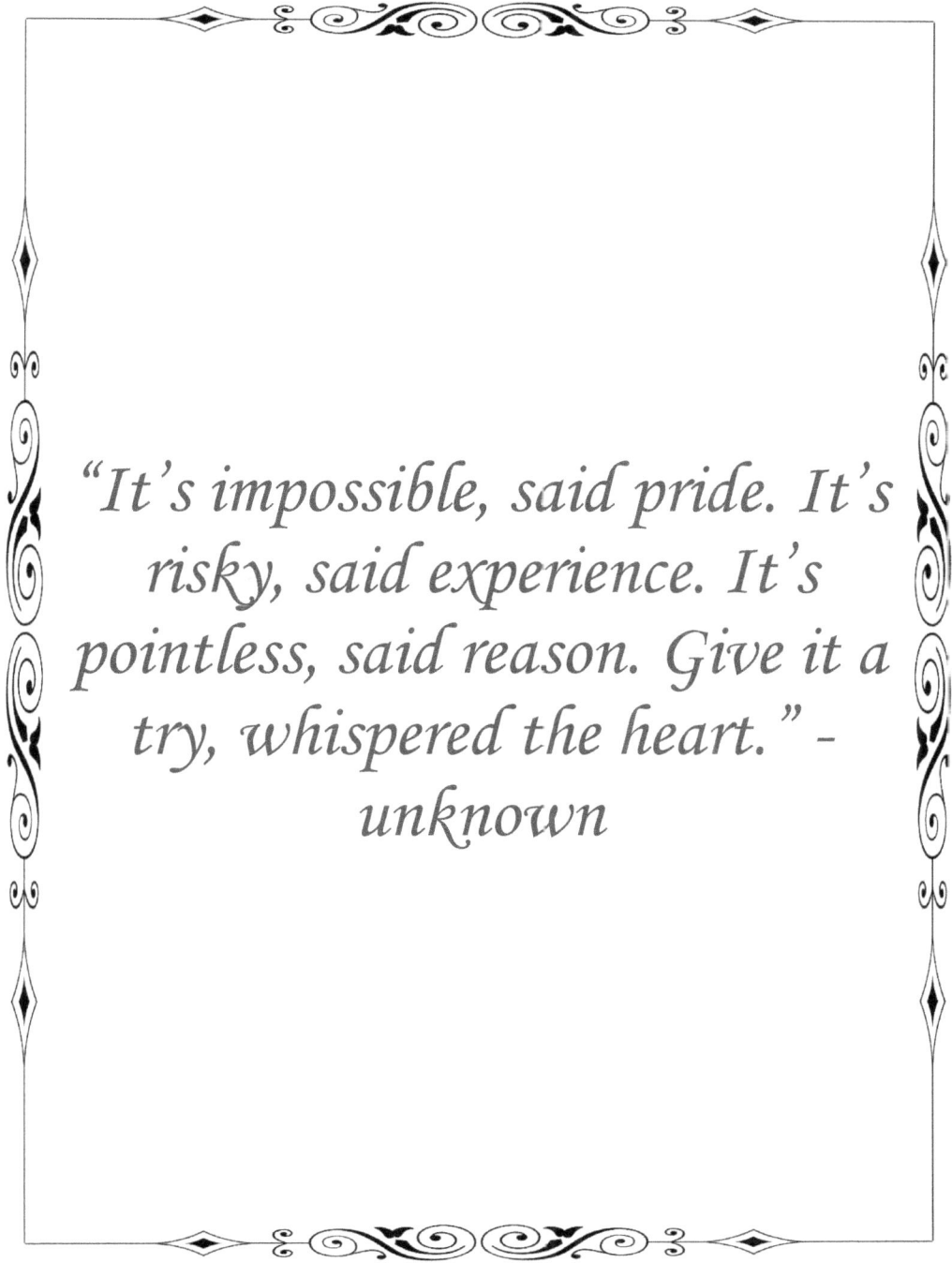

"It's impossible, said pride. It's risky, said experience. It's pointless, said reason. Give it a try, whispered the heart." - unknown

Your Daily Motivational Quote
Day 311

"There are always flowers for those who want to see them." - Henri Matisse

Your Daily Motivational Quote
Day 312

"No snowflake ever falls in the wrong place." -zen saying

Your Daily Motivational Quote
Day 313

"Have big dreams. You will grow into them." -unknown

Your Daily Motivational Quote
Day 314

"A single sunbeam is enough to drive away many shadows." -St. Francis of Assisi

Your Daily Motivational Quote
Day 315

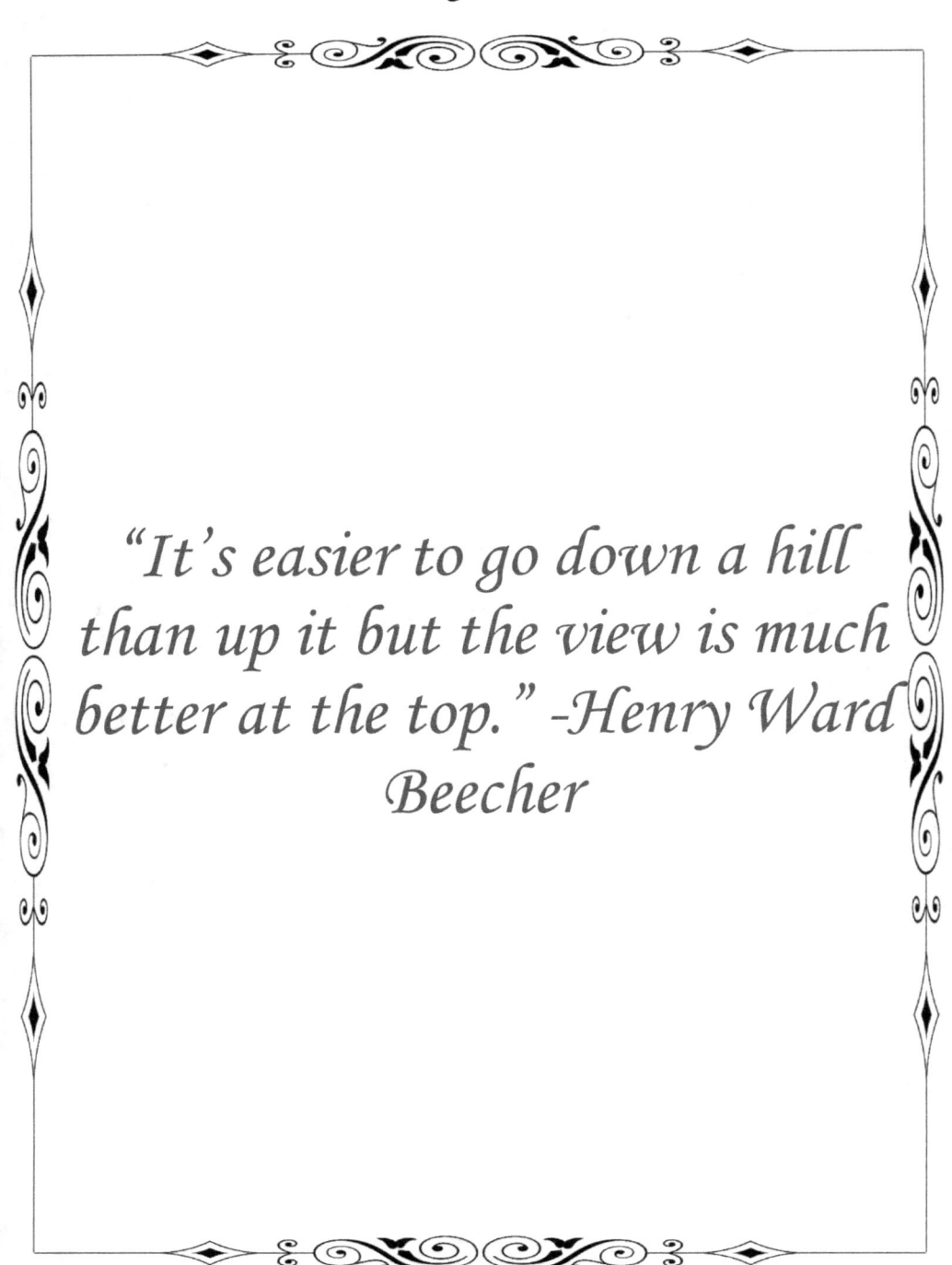

"It's easier to go down a hill than up it but the view is much better at the top." -Henry Ward Beecher

Your Daily Motivational Quote
Day 316

"Home is the nicest word there is." -Laura Ingalls Wilder

Your Daily Motivational Quote
Day 317

"There is a kind of beauty in imperfection." -Conrad Hall

Your Daily Motivational Quote
Day 318

"One of the most sincere forms of respect is actually listening to what another has to say." - Bryant H. McGill

Your Daily Motivational Quote
Day 319

"The only thing you take with you when you're gone is what you leave behind." -John Allston

Your Daily Motivational Quote
Day 320

"People will stare. Make it worth their while." -Harry Winston

Your Daily Motivational Quote
Day 321

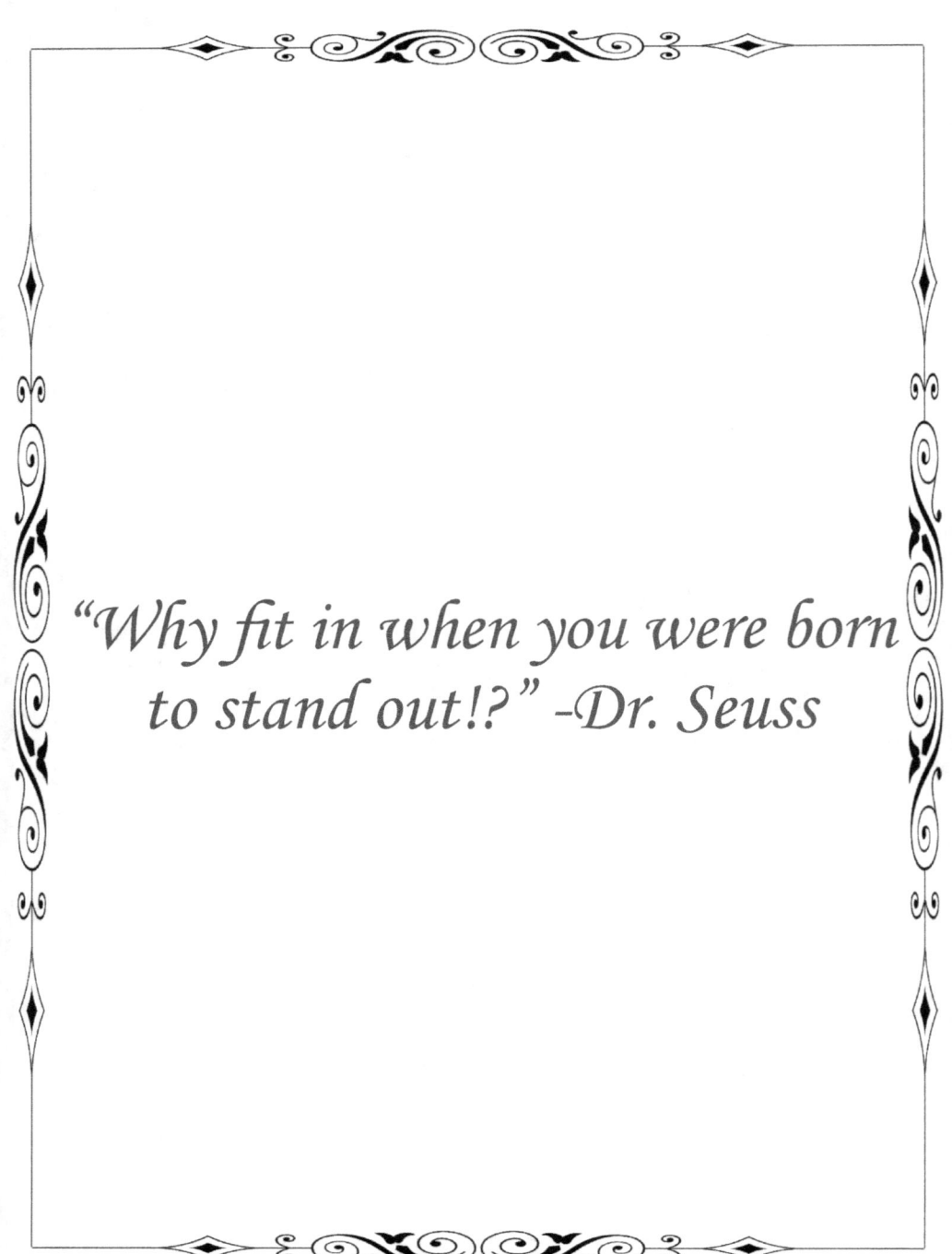

"Why fit in when you were born to stand out!?" -Dr. Seuss

Your Daily Motivational Quote
Day 322

"Do not wait until the conditions are perfect to begin. Beginning makes the conditions perfect." -unknown

Your Daily Motivational Quote
Day 323

"Happiness is having a scratch for every itch." -Ogden Nash

Your Daily Motivational Quote
Day 324

"The color of springtime is in the flowers; the color of winter is in the imagination." -Terri Guillemets

Your Daily Motivational Quote
Day 325

"I know of nothing more valuable, when it comes to the all-important virtue of authenticity, than simply being who you are." -Charles R. Swindoll

Your Daily Motivational Quote
Day 326

"A heart that loves is always young." -Greek proverb

Your Daily Motivational Quote
Day 327

"The holiday season is a perfect time to reflect on our blessings and seek out ways to make life better for those around us." - Terri Marshall

Your Daily Motivational Quote
Day 328

"It is our choices that show us who we truly are far more than our abilities." -Albus Dumbledore

Your Daily Motivational Quote
Day 329

"Nothing can dim the light that shines from within." -Maya Angelou

Your Daily Motivational Quote
Day 330

"I've learned through the years that it's not where you live, it's the people who surround you that make you feel at home." - J.B. McGee

Your Daily Motivational Quote
Day 331

"Deep in their roots, all flowers keep the light." -Theodore Roethke

Your Daily Motivational Quote
Day 332

"Some of us think holding on makes us strong but sometimes it is letting go." -Hermann Hesse

Your Daily Motivational Quote
Day 333

"Those who have the ability to be grateful are the ones who have the ability to achieve greatness."
-Steve Maraboli

Your Daily Motivational Quote
Day 334

"In time, lies bring turmoil, where honesty brings peace." - Wes Fesler

Your Daily Motivational Quote
Day 335

"Patience allows life time to fall in place." -An Iota of Truth

Your Daily Motivational Quote
Day 336

"If you judge people, you have no time to love them." -Mother Teresa

Your Daily Motivational Quote
Day 337

"A good life is a collection of happy moments." -Denis Waitley

Your Daily Motivational Quote
Day 338

"There is nothing more truly artistic than to love people." - Vincent Van Gogh

Your Daily Motivational Quote
Day 339

"Coming together is a beginning. Keeping together is progress. Working together is success." - Henry Ford

Your Daily Motivational Quote
Day 340

"As soon as I saw you, I knew an adventure was going to happen." -Winnie the Pooh

Your Daily Motivational Quote
Day 341

"The best time to plant a tree was twenty years ago. The next best time is today." -proverb

Your Daily Motivational Quote
Day 342

"Color! What a deep and mysterious language, the language of dreams." -Paul Gauguin

Your Daily Motivational Quote
Day 343

"Art is not what you see, but what you make others see." - Edgar Degas

Your Daily Motivational Quote
Day 344

"Protect what you love." - unknown

Your Daily Motivational Quote
Day 345

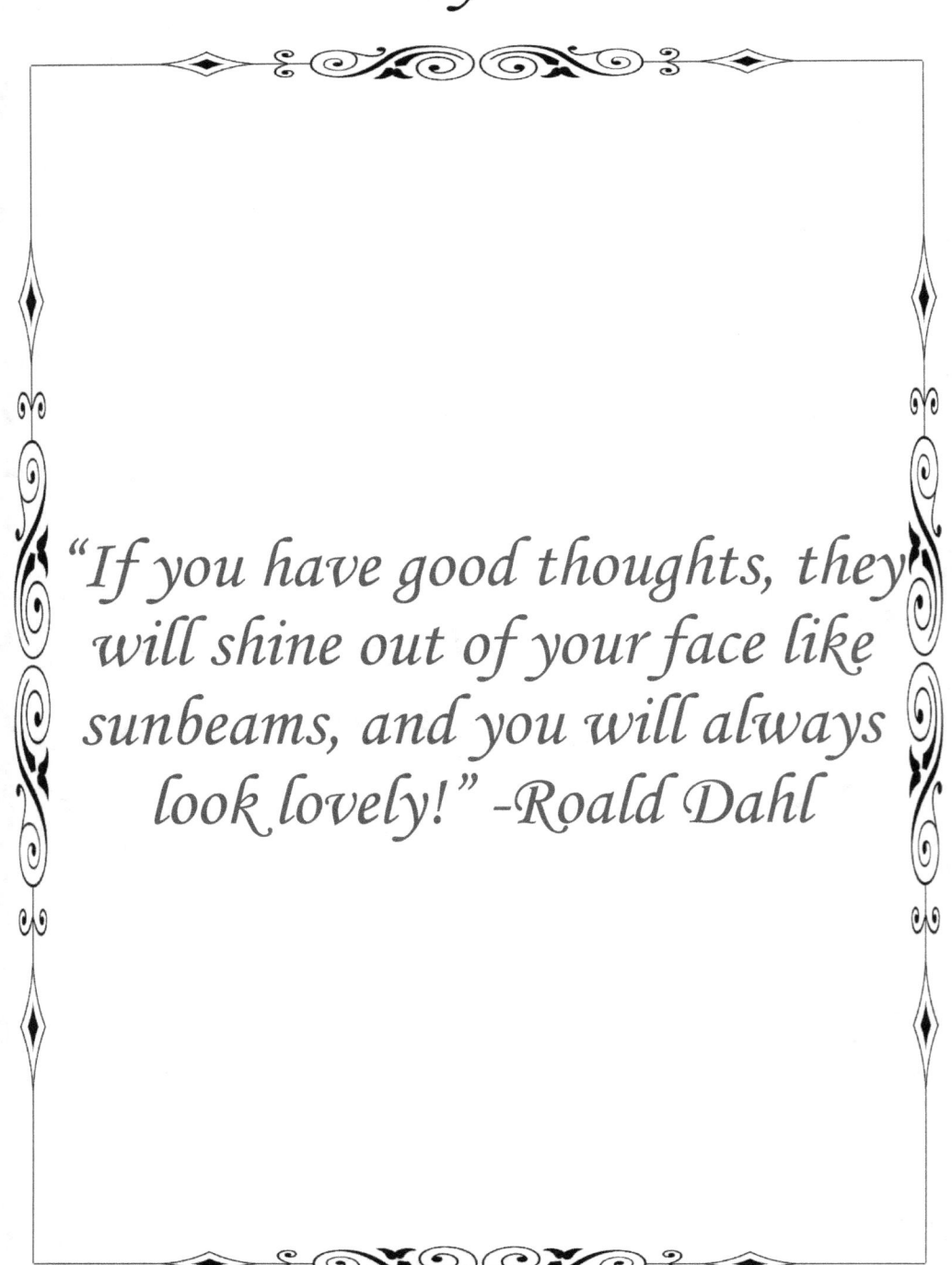

"If you have good thoughts, they will shine out of your face like sunbeams, and you will always look lovely!" -Roald Dahl

Your Daily Motivational Quote
Day 346

"Create with the heart; build with the mind." -Criss Jami

Your Daily Motivational Quote
Day 347

"The world breaks every one and afterward many are strong at the broken places." -Ernest Hemingway

Your Daily Motivational Quote
Day 348

"Don't let life discourage you; everyone who got where he is had to begin where he was." - Richard L. Evans

Your Daily Motivational Quote
Day 349

"Because when you stop and look around, this life is pretty amazing." -Dr.Seuss

Your Daily Motivational Quote
Day 350

"Home is people. Not a place. If you go back there after the people are gone, then all you can see is what is not there any more." -Robin Hobb

Your Daily Motivational Quote
Day 351

"The best part about pictures is that even when the people in the photo change, the memory it contains never will." -unknown

Your Daily Motivational Quote
Day 352

"Without forgiveness, there's no future." -Desmond Tutu

Your Daily Motivational Quote
Day 353

"Change will not come if we wait for some other person, or if we wait for some other time. We are the ones we've been waiting for. We are the change that we seek."
-Barack Obama

Your Daily Motivational Quote
Day 354

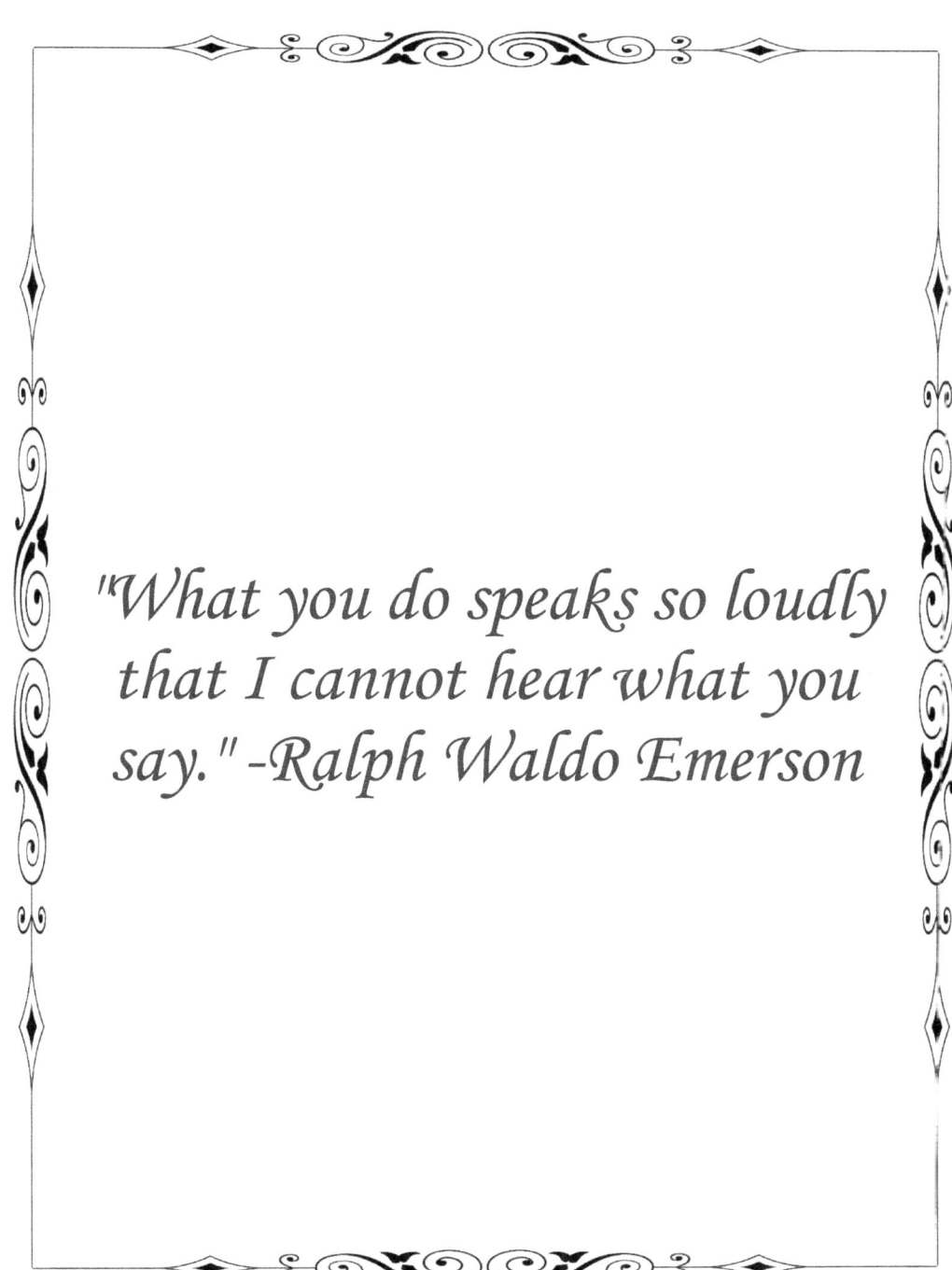

"What you do speaks so loudly that I cannot hear what you say." -Ralph Waldo Emerson

Your Daily Motivational Quote
Day 355

"The slogans "hang on" and "press on" have solved and will continue to solve the problems of humanity." -Ogwo David Emenike

Your Daily Motivational Quote
Day 356

"Every sunrise is an invitation for us to arise and brighten someone's day." -Richelle E. Goodrich

Your Daily Motivational Quote
Day 357

"Truth is a deep kindness that teaches us to be content in our everyday life and share with the people the same happiness." - Khalil Gibran

Your Daily Motivational Quote
Day 358

"When you are grateful-when you can see what you have-you unlock blessings to flow in your life."-Suze Orman

Your Daily Motivational Quote
Day 359

"Simplicity is the most difficult thing to secure in this world; it is the last limit of experience and the last effort of genius." -George Sand

Your Daily Motivational Quote
Day 360

"People tend to play in their comfort zone, so the best things are achieved in a state of surprise, actually." -Brian Eno

Your Daily Motivational Quote
Day 361

It is the soul's duty to be loyal to its own desires. It must abandon itself to its master passion. - Rebecca West

Your Daily Motivational Quote
Day 362

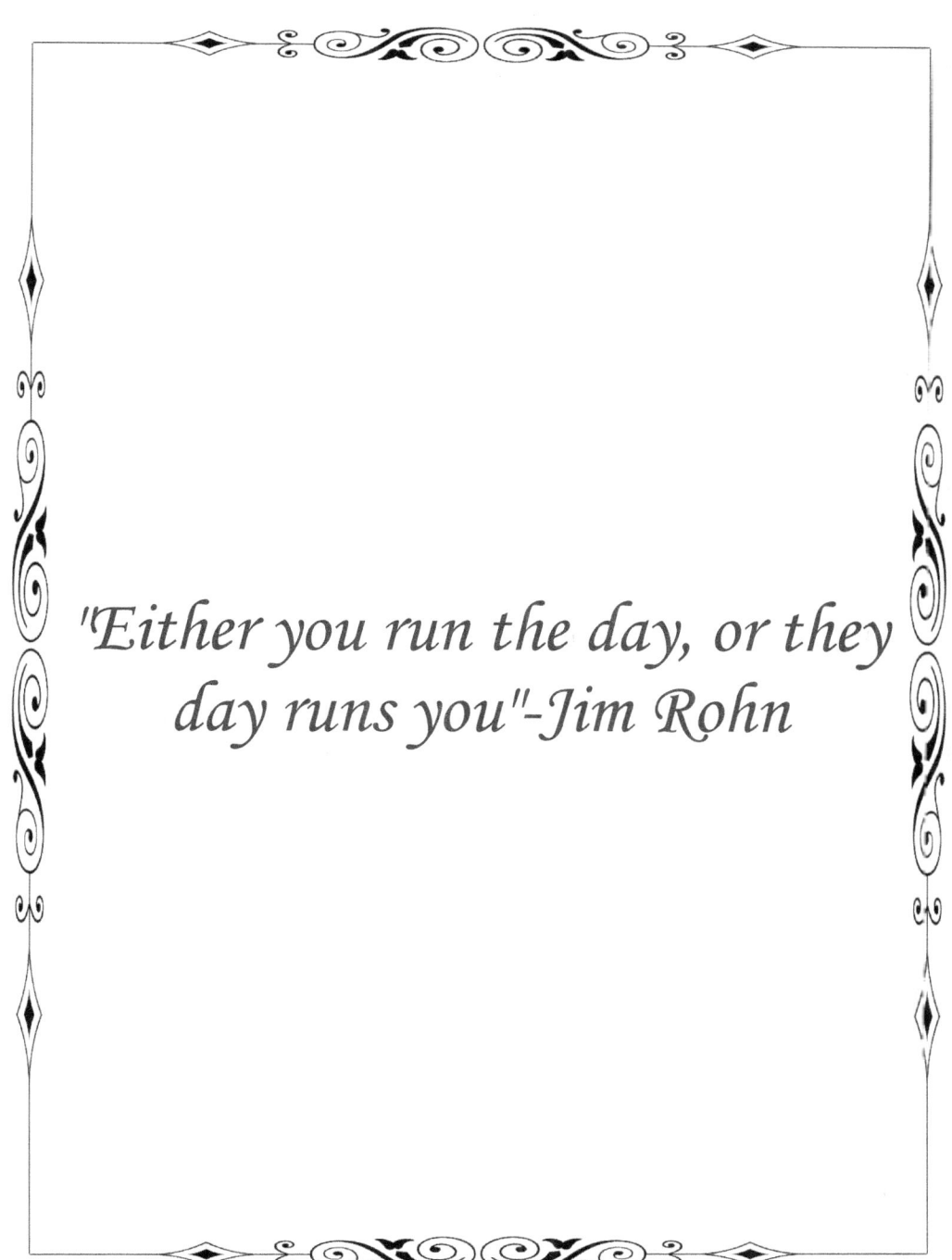

"Either you run the day, or they day runs you"-Jim Rohn

Your Daily Motivational Quote
Day 363

"Unity is strength. . . when there is teamwork and collaboration, wonderful things can be achieved." -Mattie Stepanek

Your Daily Motivational Quote
Day 364

"He had shown her all the workings of his soul, mistaking this for love." -E.M. Forster

Your Daily Motivational Quote
Day 365

"The price of anything is the amount of life you exchange for it." -Henry David Thoreau